The Gospel According to Christ's Enemies

THE BANNER OF TRUTH TRUST

Head Office
3 Murrayfield Road
Edinburgh, EH12 6EL
UK

North America Office
PO Box 621
Carlisle, PA 17013
USA

banneroftruth.org

First published 2022
© David J. Randall 2022

*

ISBN
Print: 978 1 80040 253 9
Epub: 978 1 80040 254 6
Kindle: 978 1 80040 255 3

*

Typeset in 11/15 pt Adobe Garamond Pro at
The Banner of Truth Trust, Edinburgh

Printed in the USA by
Versa Press Inc.,
East Peoria, IL.

The Gospel
According to
Christ's Enemies

Unintended Statements of Saving Truth

David J. Randall

THE BANNER OF TRUTH TRUST

Contents

The soldiers twisted together a crown of thorns
and put it on his head

John 19:2

Introduction:
Jesus and His Enemies

The New Testament begins with the four gospels of Matthew, Mark, Luke, and John. They wrote their accounts of the life, teaching, death, and resurrection of Jesus Christ, and if we accept the common belief that the Gospel of Mark is the earliest, then the first recorded words of Jesus[1] refer to 'the gospel': 'After John was arrested, Jesus came into Galilee, proclaiming the gospel of God, and saying, "The time is fulfilled, and the kingdom of God is at hand; repent and believe in the gospel"' (Mark 1:14, 15).

In the above paragraph, the word gospel is used in two senses. It refers to each of the four written accounts and it also describes the one message to which all the gospel writers bear witness. F. F. Bruce pointed out that the plural form 'gospels' would not have been understood in the first century:

> It is of the essence of the apostolic witness that there is only one true euangelion... The four records which tradition-ally stand in the forefront of the New Testament are properly

---

[1] Apart from his enigmatic words at the age of twelve when Mary and Joseph found him in the temple discussing matters with the religious leaders there: 'Why were you looking for me? Did you not know that I must be in my Father's house?' (Luke 2:49).

speaking, four records of the one gospel—'the gospel of God…
concerning his Son' (Romans 1:1-3). It was not until the middle
of the second century AD that the plural form came to be used.[2]

The word is found in its varying forms about seventy-five times
in the New Testament and nearly every time[3] it refers to the
one gospel message that is centred in Jesus Christ, especially his
death and resurrection. It is this one gospel that all of the writers
sought to proclaim and spread. 'Him we proclaim,' wrote the
apostle Paul (Col. 1:28), and towards the end of his life he asked
for prayer 'that words may be given to me in opening my mouth
boldly to proclaim the mystery of the gospel, for which I am an
ambassador in chains…' (Eph. 6:19, 20).

This gospel is the good news of salvation that comes through
faith in Jesus Christ and it was the aim of all the writers of Scripture to bring people to faith. The apostle John expressed this aim
when, after mentioning that many things were said and done
by Jesus which have not been recorded, he wrote: 'but these are
written so that you may believe that Jesus is the Christ, the Son of
God, and that by believing you may have life in his name' (John
20:30, 31).

All twenty-seven books of the New Testament were written by
people who believed in him and were committed to the exten-
sion of his kingdom. However, there were several occasions when
hostile people gave unintended expression to the truth of the one
gospel. That is the subject of this book: the gospel—according to
Christ's enemies.

A common expression says, 'Many a true word is spoken in
jest.'[4] The sayings highlighted in this book were not spoken as

---

[2] *Illustrated Bible Dictionary*, Part 2 (Leicester: IVP, 1980), 581.
[3] Other than two uses to refer to 'another' (i.e. false) gospel (2 Cor. 11:4; Gal. 1:6).
[4] Attributed to Shakespeare and to Chaucer before him.

jokes (except possibly the statement considered in chapter 8, where the name 'Christian' may have been partly a jest) but many a true word is also spoken in irony—when people's words signify more that they intended.

The expressions to be considered here were uttered by people who had their own agendas, their own reasons for saying what they said, but their words point to deeper truths than they intended.

Double meanings

People sometimes say things that unintentionally carry double meanings. It is the stuff of jokes—people take something out of someone else's words which the speaker didn't have in mind at all. For example, a man is at a Christian meeting where people are invited to come forward for prayer about things that bother them. This man comes forward and when the preacher asks what he wants prayer for, he asks prayer for his hearing. So the preacher places his hands on the man's ears and prays fervently for his hearing. Afterwards he asks the man if his hearing is okay and is told, 'I don't know; it isn't until next Tuesday'![5]

C. S. Lewis wrote of another kind of double meaning. He was writing about the Psalms of the Old Testament and the way in which they have a meaning in their original context and also a deeper meaning when seen as part of the completed Bible and in light of the ministry of Jesus.

In that context, he told this fascinating story:

> One of the Roman historians tells us about a fire in a provin-
> cial town which was thought to have originated in the public

---

[5] A hearing is a legal proceeding before a judge or magistrate, in which evidence and argument are presented to determine the facts of a case and how it should proceed.

baths. What gave some colour to the suspicion of deliberate incendiarism was the fact that, earlier that day, a gentleman had complained that the water in the hot bath was only luke-warm and had received from an attendant the reply, it will soon be hot enough. Now of course if there really had been a plot, and the slave was in it, and fool enough to risk discovery by this veiled threat, then the story would not concern us. But let us suppose the fire was an accident (i.e. was intended by nobody). In that case the slave would have said something truer, or more importantly true, than he himself supposed. Clearly, there need be nothing here but chance coincidence. The slave's reply is fully explained by the customer's complaint; it is just what any bath attendant would say. The deeper significance which his words turned out to have during the next few hours was, as we should say, accidental.[6]

In the case of Scriptural words, however, which the Bible itself claims were inspired ('breathed out') by God (2 Tim. 3:16), there may well be more to matters than simple coincidence. In one case which we shall consider, the apostle John specifically says about a statement made by the high priest of the time, 'He did not say this of his own accord, but being high priest that year he *prophesied* that Jesus would die for the nation' (John 11:51; my emphasis).

That is one of the several expressions of the gospel according to Christ's enemies that we will consider:

- First there are the words of his critics in Luke 15:2—'This man receives sinners.'

- Then the report of some soldiers sent by Christ's enemies to arrest him. They came back empty-handed and said, 'No one ever spoke like this man' (John 7:46).

- There is the occasion when Caiaphas said it would be more

---

[6] *Reflections on the Psalms* (Glasgow: Geoffrey Bles, 1958), 85.

expedient that one man (Jesus) should die rather than the whole nation be eliminated by the Romans (John 11:50).

- Pontius Pilate said to the crowds about Jesus, 'Behold your King.'

- As Jesus hung on the cross, the chief priests and the teachers of the law mocked him; they said, 'He saved others, but he can't save himself!' (Mark 15:31).

- Later, Paul, the one-time enemy of Christ, came to regard it as 'trustworthy and deserving of full acceptance, that Christ Jesus came into the world to save sinners' (1 Tim. 1:15).

- Acts tells us that in Antioch 'the disciples were first called Christians' (Acts 11:26) and, whether that was said with enmity, mockery or indifference, we shall consider the people of Antioch's words as testifying to the gospel.

- In Acts 17:6 we find the accusation that the apostles, in proclaiming the gospel, were 'turning the world upside down.'

- Last, in Athens, Paul was dismissed as a 'babbler' who was presenting new teaching (Acts 17:18, 19).

As we consider these unintentional statements of gospel truth by Christ's enemies, it is interesting to consider them in the context of his attitude toward his enemies.

Jesus and his enemies

It is well known that Jesus spoke about loving one's enemies: 'You have heard that it was said, "You shall love your neighbour and hate your enemy." But I say to you, "Love your enemies…"' (Matt. 5:44).

He had referred to other things that people had read in and heard from the Old Testament, but it was not in the Old Testament that they read or heard anything about hating their enemies.[7] In fact, the Old Testament says, 'You shall love your neighbour as yourself' (Lev. 19:18), and it seems that the scribes and others had drawn the unwarranted inference that loving your neighbour involves hating your enemy. Jesus was teaching an entirely different way: instead of hating your enemies, love them.

And he practised what he preached. It is true that he could speak strong words, notably against religious hypocrisy (see, for example, Matt. 23), but his words, even when strong, were not spoken in hatred. The Bible itself says, 'Faithful are the wounds of a friend' (Prov. 27:6). Real love is ready to say the difficult things that need to be said, and Jesus' whole life was characterised by love for other people, including his enemies. As an infrequently-sung hymn says:

> What grace, O Lord, and beauty shone
>> Around Thy steps below.
> What patient love was seen in all
>> Thy life and death of woe.
>
> For ever on Thy burdened heart
>> A weight of sorrow hung,
> Yet no ungentle, murmuring word
>> Escaped Thy silent tongue.

---

[7] Such a thing *was* written in one of the manuscripts of the Essene community discovered in 1947 at Qumran. Their *Community Rule* (known as 1QS) says that the leader should 'admit into the Covenant of Grace all those who have freely devoted themselves to the observance of God's precepts, that they may be joined to the counsel of God and… that they may love all the sons of light, each according to his lot in God's design, and hate all the sons of darkness, each according to his guilt in God's vengeance.' Geza Vermes, *The Dead Sea Scrolls in English* (Harmondsworth: Penguin Books, 1962), 72.

> Thy foes might hate, despise, revile,
> Thy friends unfaithful prove;
> Unwearied in forgiveness still,
> Thy heart could only love.[8]

The time when we learn most about Jesus' attitude to his enemies is the time of his death. Crucifixion must have been a fearfully awful way to be put to death. It would normally be preceded by severe physical assault, and the pain of being nailed to a wooden stake and left to die slowly from blood loss and asphyxiation is beyond imagining. Yet we hear Jesus, in one of his seven recorded sayings from the cross, praying, 'Father, forgive them, for they know not what they do' (Luke 23:34).

In one sense they did know. His enemies had planned and engineered this event for a long time and they must have been greatly relieved that they seemed to have finally had their way. They were getting rid of a troublemaker.

Yet, at a deeper level, they did not know what they were doing; they didn't realise that this crucifixion was at the heart of God's eternal plan of salvation. They had no idea that it was through this death, this sacrificial death, that God's forgiveness and salvation would become realities. Christ was giving his life as a ransom for many (Mark 10:45), such that, years later, Peter wrote to believers as those who were 'ransomed from the futile ways inherited from your forefathers, not with perishable things such as silver and gold, but with the precious blood of Christ, like that of a lamb without blemish or spot.' (1 Peter 1:18, 19).

His enemies didn't know what they were doing, and often, they didn't know what they were saying. Their attacks on him conveyed unintended things about his teaching, his impact, his welcome of 'sinners,' his substitutionary death, his revolutionary

[8] Hymn, 'What Grace' by Edward Denny (1796–1889).

gospel, and his effect on the lives of his people; including one who would write, 'I have been crucified with Christ. It is no longer I who live, but Christ who lives in me. And the life I now live in the flesh I live by faith in the Son of God, who loved me and gave himself for me.' (Gal. 2:20).

The apostle Paul was nothing if not enthusiastic in his service for Christ; he devoted all his energies of body, mind, and spirit to the service of Christ and his kingdom. If ever a person lived out the words of the hymn that says, 'Take my voice and let me sing always, only, for my King' and 'Take my intellect and use every power as Thou shalt choose,'[9] that person was Paul. He was second to none in his enthusiasm for Christ's service.

Interestingly, that word *enthusiasm* was once used as an insult. Normally nowadays, if someone is described as enthusiastic about something, that is regarded as a positive, even commendable thing, but in earlier times the word was used dismissively. To describe someone as an enthusiast was to dismiss him or her as a religious extremist. Indeed, this is how Paul came across to the Roman governor Festus.

When Paul was telling King Agrippa and Festus about his conversion, Festus burst out at one point, 'Paul, you are out of your mind' (Acts 26:24). He recognised Paul's eloquence and intelligence but he said, 'Your great learning is driving you out of your mind'—anticipating Dryden's lines:

> Great wits are sure to madness near allied
> And thin partitions do their bounds divide.[10]

To that we might well respond by saying that if Paul was mad, it would be good if we were all mad! As for this kind of enthusiasm,

[9] Hymn, 'Take my life' by Frances Ridley Harvergal (1836–79).
[10] *Absalom and Achitophel* by John Dryden (1631–1700).

surely we need more of it and less of the attitude found in the days of George Whitefield (1714–70):

> There was, however, one aspect of the religious question on which the people of England were in general unity. This was the fear of what they called 'enthusiasm'. The term meant as much or more than the word 'fanatic' today,[11] and they applied it to anyone whose practice of Christianity manifested any true fervour… public opinion decreed that everything to do with religion must be quietly dispassionate. Thus, empty formality was the order of the day, and an unwritten law demanded that it remain so.[12]

Whitefield had no truck with such a notion. Much more importantly, neither did Jesus who said we are to love the Lord with all our heart and soul and mind (Matt. 22:37).

In George Bernard Shaw's play about Joan of Arc there is a scene in which someone expresses his willingness to pay out sixteen francs for a horse for Joan because 'her words and her ardent faith in God have put fire into me.' His companion says, 'Whew! You are as mad as she is,' and he responds, 'We want a few mad people now. See where the sane ones have landed us!'[13]

Paul responded to the charge that he was insane by saying, 'I am not out of my mind, most excellent Festus, but I am speaking true and reasonable words' (Acts 26:25). The gospel of Christ brings sense and sanity to a mad world, and as we reflect on that gospel we can find instruction even in the gospel according to Christ's enemies.

---

[11] Many people today would happily accept the description of themselves as 'fans' of a football team or film star, without recalling that 'fan' is short for 'fanatic.' For many, it's fine to be keenly enthusiastic about sport or a pop group (even devoted fans) but when it comes to religious devotion, that's a different matter!

[12] A. Dallimore, *George Whitefield* Vol. 1 (London: Banner of Truth, 1970), 23-4.

[13] G. B. Shaw, *Saint Joan* (London: Constable & Co., 1926), 6.

2

He Welcomes Sinners!

Controversy was never far from Jesus during the days of his earthly ministry. When John says, in the first chapter of his gospel, that Jesus came to his own but his own did not receive him (John 1:11), he uncovers one of the most striking ironies of Jesus' ministry. The Jews, the very people who should have been most ready to welcome him, rejected him instead.

Later in his gospel, John writes, 'Though he had done so many signs before them, they still did not believe in him' (John 12:37), and of course that rejection culminated in the crucifixion which was principally engineered by the Jewish leaders. Despite centuries of national preparation, they rejected their Messiah when he came in the flesh.

However, the four gospels also tell us that the Jewish rejection of Jesus was by no means universal. The other part of John's statement in John 1 acknowledges this: 'But to all who did receive him, who believed in his name, he gave the right to become children of God' (John 1:12).

Jesus' chief adversaries were the leaders of the people—those who were most familiar with the prophecies that were being fulfilled in Jesus. In contrast, the gospel writers bring before us many instances of the *common people* hearing him gladly (Mark 12:37). In particular there were people who were often despised and rejected by others, people like the 'tax collectors and sinners' mentioned at the beginning of Luke 15, a chapter which brings before us a remarkable example of the gospel expressed by Christ's enemies.

Luke's account begins, 'Now the tax collectors and sinners were all drawing near to hear him. And the Pharisees and the scribes grumbled, saying, "This man receives sinners and eats with them." So he told them this parable...' (Luke 15:1-3). The chapter goes on to record the three parables of the lost sheep, the lost coin and the lost sons. But this was the criticism levelled at him: 'This man receives sinners.' If ever there was a backhanded compliment...

In that simple statement is an unintended expression of wonderful truth. In Greek it consists of only three words: 'This welcomes sinners'—which (at least in English) seems to give expression to the contempt with which the speakers regarded Jesus in His willingness to associate with such people.

He receives sinners!

It is true! This man does receive and welcome sinners—and thank God for that, because it is our only hope. As an old hymn says, 'Sinners Jesus will receive: Tell this word of grace to all'; and the last verse of the hymn says:

> Christ receiveth sinful men,
>   Even me with all my sin;
> Openeth to me heaven again;
>   With Him I may enter in.
> Death hath no more sting or pain:
>   Christ receiveth sinful men.[1]

[1] Hymn, 'Sinners Jesus will receive' by Erdmann Neumeister (1671–1756). (Here 'men' refers to all humans.)

A Scottish minister was once invited to preach in a colleague's church and afterwards the local minister commented, 'That was a very good sermon, I suppose, but it was unsuitable here; for you spoke all day to sinners, and I know of only one in all my parish'![2] Fortunate parish! Did he mean to distinguish between unrepentant sinners and the repentant sinners of his parish who were trusting (all but one) in Christ as their Saviour? If so, again—fortunate parish. But one suspects that he was making an assumption that all the decent law-abiding people in his parish shouldn't have been classed as 'sinners.' They were too respectable for that!

The Pharisees and scribes had apparently been keeping an eye on Jesus, this controversial teacher from Nazareth, who seemed to them to be getting ideas above his station. They regarded themselves as the custodians of true religion and morality, and they may have thought, 'who is this new kid on the block to be going around saying the things he is saying and doing the things he is doing?'

There was no doubt he was causing a stir; indeed, there was no doubt that he had a growing popularity with many of the 'ordinary' people, and these religious leaders didn't like it. So, when they attacked him for associating with tax collectors and sinners, they were expressing their contempt for him. They were saying, 'Anyone can see that he can't be much of a holy man if these are the kind of people who are drawn to him!'

In this chapter we will consider the sinners, the man, and the welcome.

The sinners

Luke tells us that the critics of Jesus took issue with his association with the tax collectors in particular, and sinners in general.

---

[2] Recounted in Iain H. Murray, *A Scottish Christian Heritage* (Edinburgh: Banner of Truth, 2006), 120.

It is well known that tax collectors were, to put it mildly, disliked by most people. They were regarded as traitors, men who were prepared to do the Romans' dirty work for them. Most Jews hated being under the rule of Rome, they hated having to pay taxes to Caesar, and they hated those who collected these taxes. To get the flavour of how they were regarded, we might think about the way in which loan sharks and drug pushers are regarded by most people nowadays.

Yet the tax collectors were finding in Jesus a listening ear, a welcoming attitude, and, most wonderfully of all, a redeeming influence. Two notable tax collectors are described in some detail in the gospels.

One was Matthew, the gospel writer. The critics of Jesus could now see Matthew going around as one of Jesus' disciples, enthused about the gospel and keen to bring others into God's Kingdom.

It was an amazing turnaround. A few chapters earlier, the Gospel of Luke had told of Jesus seeing Matthew (a.k.a. Levi) sitting at his tax booth and, whether Matthew had already been attracted to Jesus or not, it simply says that Jesus called to him, 'Follow me', and, 'Leaving everything, he rose and followed him' (Luke 5:27, 28).

Matthew then threw a party and there was a large company of tax collectors and others reclining at table with them. And on that occasion the Pharisees and scribes 'grumbled at his disciples, saying, "Why do you eat and drink with tax collectors and sinners?"'

It says that they directed their attack at the disciples, but Jesus heard what they said, and he responded, 'Those who are well have no need of a physician, but those who are sick. I have not come to call the righteous but sinners to repentance' (Luke 5:29-32). By 'the righteous' he clearly meant those who *think* they are righteous and assume that they have no need of forgiveness and salvation—the kind of person who left a certain church after listening to the preaching of a new minister for a year and gave as her reason, 'This man preaches to us as if we were sinners'![3] The Pharisees and scribes thought like that.

They appear again in connection with another famous tax collector, little Zacchaeus. Zacchaeus is introduced as 'a chief tax collector and rich' (Luke 19:2). He was also famously short in height and climbed a tree to see Jesus, who stopped and engaged Zacchaeus in conversation. And when Jesus actually entered Zacchaeus' house, we are told that they again 'grumbled, "He has gone in to be the guest of a man who is a sinner."'

But something had happened in the tax collector's heart; we might like to know more about what happened before and after the encounter, but we are told that Zacchaeus' changed heart was shown immediately in his statement that he intended to give half of his goods to the poor and restore fourfold anything he had taken from other people by fraud (Luke 19:8).

The story ends with Jesus saying to him, 'Today salvation has come to this house, since he also is a son of Abraham. For the Son of man came to seek and to save the lost' (Luke 19:9-10).

This was in fact the gospel message, unwittingly expressed by the Pharisees and scribes of Luke 15:2. The New International Version, in the first words of the chapter, puts the word 'sinners' in inverted commas, attempting to convey something of the sneer behind the word as used by the Pharisees. They didn't regard themselves as included in that category; the sinners were

---

[3] Martyn Lloyd-Jones, *Preaching and Preachers* (London: Hodder & Stoughton, 1972), 149.

the 'riff-raff' whose lives didn't match *their* standard of meticulous rectitude and respectability.

It is not that the Pharisees were bad people. They have had rather a bad press, but they *were* people who tried hard to obey all the details of the law of Moses—and much else besides. It was not the intensity of their efforts that was suspect, but the fact that they concentrated on outward appearances. The famous cartoon-like description about straining out a gnat while swallowing a camel (Matt. 23:24) was Jesus' characterisation of them; as my Study Bible says, they had 'become lost in the details, while neglecting the law's major purposes.'[4]

I once read about a Bible college that advertised itself as being 'seven miles from any known form of sin'! Presumably they meant that there were no casinos, brothels or drinking dens anywhere near them, but the truth is that you can't get seven miles from sin, because sin is in the human heart.

As Jesus said on another occasion and in connection with another controversy (concerning ritual hand-washing), 'for out of the heart come evil thoughts, murder, adultery, sexual immorality, theft, false witness, slander. These are what defile a person' (Matt. 15:19, 20).

That 'out of the heart' highlights the problem of thinking you can get seven miles from sin and it highlights the issue behind all of Jesus' controversies with the Pharisees. If only they would have faced the reality of sin in their hearts, not only in their outward deeds—as indeed one notable Pharisee did. I refer to the apostle Paul who pointed out in Acts 23:6 and 26:5 that he 'according to the strictest party of our religion, lived as a Pharisee' and was 'educated at the feet of Gamaliel according to the strict manner of the law of our fathers, being zealous for God' (Acts 22:3).

[4] *ESV Student Study Bible* (London: HarperCollins, 2011), 1,282.

But Paul came to realise that no amount of outward adherence to the law and no amount of good deeds could make him right with God. We might say that the Pharisees' charge in Luke 15:2—'this man receives sinners'—is seconded by Paul; only, in his case it was no criticism but a statement of the good news. 'The saying is trustworthy and deserving of full acceptance, that Christ Jesus came into the world to save sinners, of whom I am the foremost' (1 Tim. 1:15). Far from denying that he was a sinner, he regarded himself as the chief of sinners and for him the fact that Jesus welcomes sinners was no criticism but the most wonderful truth.

He went on, 'But I received mercy for this reason, that in me, as the foremost, Jesus Christ might display his perfect patience as an example to those who were to believe in him' (1 Tim. 1:16).

The gospel says—and says to sinners—

> There's a way back to God from the dark paths of sin;
>   There's a door that is open and you may go in:
> At Calvary's cross is where you begin
>   When you come as a sinner to Jesus.[5]

In the eleventh century, the theologian Anselm wrote a book called *Cur Deus Homo?* (*Why did God Become Man?*). Some people criticised his teaching about the necessity of Christ's atoning death at Calvary, and his response was, 'But you have not pondered the gravity of sin.'[6] That gravity is the background against which the meaning and significance of the cross is seen. Putting it the other way round: if you wanted to undermine the teaching of the Bible on the atonement ('That wonderful redemption, God's remedy for sin'[7]), then the thing to do would be to undermine or eradicate the whole concept of sin.

---

[5] Hymn, 'There's a way back to God' by E. H. Swinstead (died 1976).
[6] Quoted by Donald Macleod, *A Faith to Live By* (Fearn: Christian Focus, 1998), 129.
[7] From hymn, *Tell me the old, old Story*, by Arabella Catherine Hankey (1834–1911).

Such undermining is going on all around us. Many people, especially in the public media and the entertainment industry that is so pervasive and influential, promote a light view of sin, regarding it as something trivial, something to be joked about, something that doesn't matter very much.

This is a far cry from the Bible's teaching, which tells us that sin is serious in its nature (as rebellion against a holy God) and in its consequences (alienating us from God and leading to hell). The world at large refuses to consider the gravity of sin, but it is against that background that Christ's work is so vital, so effective and so wonderful.

A particularly striking exposition of the trend to downplay the significance of sin was given by an American pastor, the Reverend Joe Wright, who was asked to open a session of the Kansas Senate in prayer on 23 January 1996. Although the prayer was addressed to God and not the listening senators, they certainly got more than they bargained for. His prayer is worth quoting in full:

> Heavenly Father, we come before you today to ask your forgiveness and to seek your direction and guidance. We know your word says, 'Woe to those who call evil good' but that is what we have done. We have lost our spiritual equilibrium and inverted our values. We confess that
>
> We have ridiculed the absolute truth of your word and called it pluralism;
> We have worshipped others gods and called it multiculturalism;
> We have endorsed perversion and called it alternative lifestyle;
> We have exploited the poor and called it the lottery;
> We have neglected the needy and called it self-preservation;
> We have rewarded laziness and called it welfare;
> We have killed our unborn and called it choice;

We have shot abortionists and called it justifiable;

We have neglected to discipline our children and called it building self-esteem;

We have abused power and called it political savvy;

We have coveted our neighbor's possessions and called it ambition;

We have polluted the air with profanity and pornography and called it freedom of expression;

We have ridiculed the time-honoured values of our forefathers and called it enlightenment.

Search us, O God, and know our hearts today; cleanse us from every sin and set us free. Guide and bless these men and women who have been sent here by the people of Kansas… Grant them your wisdom to rule and by their decisions to direct us to the center of your will, we ask in the name of your Son, the living Savior, Jesus Christ. Amen.[8]

I suspect he probably hasn't been asked back again! Prayer is, of course, addressed to God, not to other people, but it was still a brave thing to do; some senators walked out during the prayer, but Mr Wright gave expression to much that is our problem today.

So many people think that sin is an old-fashioned concept, something that once bothered people but which can be safely disregarded in this enlightened age; others treat it as subject of mirth. They may sing about amazing grace 'that saved a wretch like me', but try addressing one of them personally as a sinful wretch and see what happens!

But where sin is taken seriously, and where people are ready to admit that they are sinners, there is good news even in this statement which Jesus' enemies intended as a barb: 'This man receives sinners.'

---

[8] Quoted from http://www.eaec.org/desk/joe_wright_prayer.htm (accessed 5 May 2018).

It has been estimated that about five thousand stars can be seen with the naked eye, yet none can be seen in broad daylight.[9] It is when things are dark that they become visible as they shine in their brilliance. The brilliance of the good news of the gospel is wonderful when we see it against the dark background of the sin that alienates us from our Maker. It is that sin that forms a barrier between us and God. The prophet Isaiah pointed out that the problem is not with God; he said to the people of his time, 'Your iniquities have made a separation between you and your God, and your sins have hidden his face from you so that he does not hear' (Isa. 59:1).

Thank God he does receive sinners! He invites us to come to him in repentance and faith, to come as sinners. He loves us so much that he accepts us as sinners; he also loves us so much that he doesn't want to leave us as we are, but to shed abroad his love in our hearts through the Holy Spirit (Rom. 5:5) whose fruit is love, joy, peace, patience, kindness, goodness, faithfulness, gentleness and self-control (Gal. 5:22, 23).

The Man

The Pharisees and scribes spoke of Jesus here in Luke 15 as simply 'This man' (or even, as we suggested in the previous chapter, simply 'This'), and we know from what is recorded in the gospels that they, or at least most of them, had nothing but contempt for Jesus. To them he was an upstart, a leader whose followers had gone 'over-the-top', and a blasphemer. He was also politically dangerous and they concluded that he must be stopped!

They didn't realise that he was unstoppable! In John Masefield's drama, *The Trial of Jesus*, Pontius Pilate's wife asks the centurion

[9] John Blanchard, *Unwrapped* (Darlington: Evangelical Press, 2019), 1.

in charge of the execution squad how Jesus died, and then says, 'Do you think he is dead?' The centurion says, 'No, lady, I don't,' and when she asks where he is, he answers, 'Let loose in the world, lady, where neither Roman nor Jew can stop his truths.'[10]

This is 'the Man' who, to the serious annoyance of the religious leaders, was receiving 'sinners'. His character is nicely illustrated by the titles of three books sitting side-by-side on my bookshelves, namely 'The Incomparable Christ', 'The Indispensable Christ' and 'The Inescapable Christ.'

He is *incomparable*; there is no-one else like him—never has been, is not and never will be. He is unique in every way. In the next chapter we will consider the uniqueness of his words— the temple guards reported, 'No one ever spoke like this man' (John 7:46)—and later in Luke's gospel we find testimony to the uniqueness of his character: 'Pilate said to the chief priests and the crowds, 'I find no guilt in this man'" (Luke 23:4). He may have been referring to Jesus' innocence of any crime, but it is also true that no one was able to accuse him of any sin either—try as they might! And of course some people did try. Many people had a vested interest in finding some wrong thing he had done that could be cast up against him, but they just couldn't find anything to pin on him.

He is *indispensable. The Indispensable Christ* is a book by Dr George Gunn who took his title from Jesus' words in John 15:5— 'Apart from me you can do nothing.' That was Jesus' word to his disciples, which stands as his reminder that no amount of purely human effort will achieve anything for the kingdom of God, but it is also true in the deepest sense that without him life is pointless.

[10] Quoted by G. B. Duncan, *It Could Be Your Problem* (New York: HarperCollins, 1977), 23.

There is a whole book of the Bible which expounds that theme—Ecclesiastes, with its refrain about life 'under the sun' being meaningless. And the Bible's message is that if something is to be done about the basic problem of our sin which spoils life in this good world that God has created, and if we are to find stability for our souls amid the shocks and sorrows of this life, and if we are to have hope that death is not just the final mockery of all the activity and achievements of this world, then Christ is indispensable. It is Christ and Christ alone who is the centre of Christianity, this Man who (of all the crazy things) received sinners.

He is *inescapable.* He is the One with whom we all have to do sooner or later. If not sooner, then later, a day is coming when we must appear before his judgement-seat and give account of our lives in this world and how we have responded to the message of his gospel. The title of that book (*The Inescapable Christ*) alludes to the enigmatic poet Francis Thompson's *The Hound of Heaven,* which begins with the poet running away from God.

> I fled Him, down the nights and down the days;
>   I fled Him, down the arches of the years;
> I fled Him, down the labyrinthine ways
>   Of my own mind; and in the midst of tears
>   I hid from Him.

The poem tells of the pursuit of the call of Christ who is, in truth, the life-giver, the One whose desire is not to spoil but to enrich life. The poet hears the call of that Christ:

> Whom wilt thou find to love ignoble thee
>   Save Me, save only Me?
> All which I took from thee I did but take,
>   Not for thy harms.
> But just that thou might'st seek it in my arms.

And the poem ends with the invitation of the gracious Christ. Whether the poet himself responded is unknown, but his words express the call of the Christ who welcomes sinners:

> Halts by me that footfall;
>   Is my gloom, after all,
> Shade of His hand, outstretched caressingly?
>   'Ah, fondest, blindest, weakest,
>   I am He Whom thou seekest!
>   Thou dravest love from thee, who dravest Me.'[11]

The Welcome

The accusation against Jesus was that he was welcoming 'sinners'—that truly is the good news.

A young Charlotte Elliott once said, 'I suppose I must make myself worthy to be accepted by him.' When she realised that she could come to Christ just as she was, she set it down in a hymn which has been sung thousands and thousands of times:

> Just as I am, without one plea
>   But that Thy blood was shed for me
> And that Thou bidd'st me come to Thee,
>   O Lamb of God, I come.

Another verse says:

> Just as I am, Thou wilt receive,
>   Wilt welcome, pardon, cleanse, relieve;
> Because Thy promise I believe,
>   O Lamb of God, I come.[12]

The gripe of the Pharisees in Luke 15:2 actually introduces one of the most wonderful chapters of the Bible, as Jesus proceeds to relate three parables.

---

[11] *The Hound of Heaven* by Francis Thompson (1859–1907) at www.hound-ofheaven.com/poem (accessed 13 July 2022).

[12] Hymn, 'Just as I am' by Charlotte Elliott (1789–1871).

(a) First, there is the parable of the lost sheep, which gives a picture of the good Shepherd who goes out to look for the one sheep that is lost. And the concluding comment is, 'Just so, I tell you, there will be more joy in heaven over one sinner who repents than over ninety-nine righteous persons who need no repentance' (Luke 15:7).

Jesus could sometimes be very direct; on another occasion we read, 'When the chief priests and the Pharisees heard his parables, they perceived that he was speaking about them,' (Matt. 21:45) and on this occasion they could hardly have failed to 'get it.' Jesus was referring to the Pharisees who *thought* they were righteous enough not to need repentance. No shepherd needed to go looking for *them* because they were already safely in the fold!

He made the point very strongly in another of his parables, one which is introduced by Luke with the words, 'He also told this parable to some who trusted in themselves that they were righteous, and treated others with contempt' (Luke 18:9). He drew a contrast between a self-righteous Pharisee and a penitent sinner, depicting the Pharisee as praying proudly, 'God, I thank you that I am not like other men, extortioners, unjust, adulterers, or even like this tax collector. I fast twice a week; I give tithes of all that I get' (Luke 18:11-12).

The Pharisees thought that they were obviously in a special category; they were God's elite corps! But in fact it was the despised tax-collector who simply prayed, 'God, be merciful to me, a sinner' who went home 'justified'; for, as Jesus said (Luke 14:11), 'Everyone who exalts himself will be humbled, but the one who humbles himself will be exalted' (Luke 14:11).

The Pharisees might have sympathised with some church members of a later generation, of whom it was said that 'they have a feeling it's their club and they decide who joins.' This was said in connection with the induction of a black pastor to a previously all-white church in the North American city of Atlanta. The associate minister of another church observed what was happening and said that he realised *his* church would need to do the same or it would die. 'But', he went on, 'the whites here don't want any black members. They have a feeling it's their club and they decide who joins.'[13]

The simple truth taught by Scripture is that it is *God's* church and *he* decides who joins! Of course there are procedures about formal membership of a particular congregation, but in a deeper sense it is God who adds people to his church. The point was made at the end of the second chapter of Acts where a description of the life of the early church ends with, 'And the Lord added to their number day by day those who were being saved' (Acts 2:47).

He is the One who calls people to follow him and the call is the same for everyone, whether they are tax-collectors or Pharisees, downright sinners or upright sinners—he says, 'If anyone hears my voice and opens the door, I will come in to him and eat with him, and he with me' (Rev. 3:20).

(b) Returning to Luke 15, Jesus' second parable in that chapter concerns the lost coin, with the same concluding message as the first story.

(c) And the third is the famous parable of the lost sons. The younger son impatiently asked for the share of his father's estate that would come to him eventually, and then proceeded to squander it all.

Eventually he 'came to himself' and decided to risk going back home. And if we hadn't heard the story before, we might expect

---

[13] *New York Times*, 29 June 1970.

the father to say, 'No way! Don't think you can go on like that and then come crawling back to me; you've made your bed—now you'll have to lie in it.'

But of course that is exactly the opposite of what happens in Jesus' story. 'While he was still a long way off, his father saw him and felt compassion, and ran and embraced him and kissed him' (Luke 15:20).

But then there's the elder brother! He was sulking outside while a welcome-home party took place in the house. He represents the standoffish Pharisees who hated all this talk of common sinners finding grace and salvation through Christ.

Luke 15 has thirty-two verses; if there had been a verse thirty-three, what might it have said? Would Jesus have depicted the elder brother as remaining outside, complaining, 'This man receives sinners', or as coming to realise that the message of grace was for all kinds of sinners: religious or irreligious sinners, down-and-out sinners or upwardly-mobile sinners.

But there isn't a thirty-third verse; the chapter is left open-ended, as Jesus made his appeal to people to lay aside their pride and prejudice—would they embrace the message of grace for the undeserving?

Then let's fast-forward to another day, when three crosses were set up at Calvary. Two other men were crucified alongside Jesus—criminals and rebels against Rome. And the story is familiar, as one of them comes away with his astonishing cry, breathlessly croaked no doubt from the agonies of his suffering, 'Jesus, remember me when you come into your kingdom' (Luke 23:42).

It is surely one of the most striking of all the striking sayings in the Bible. Their lives were being choked out of them—what 'kingdom' could there possibly be? Yet, despite everything in his past life of crime and violence, here was Jesus assuring him, 'Truly, I say to you, today you will be with me in Paradise.'

This man had nothing, and he certainly had no claim on God; there was nothing he could give as a reason why he should be admitted to God's heaven. I wonder whether the hymn-writer had him in mind when he wrote one of his verses—it certainly fits, some of it in the most literal way:

> Nothing in my hand I bring;
>   Simply to Thy cross I cling;
> Naked, come to Thee for dress,
>   Helpless, look to Thee for grace,
> Foul, I to the fountain fly;
>   Wash me, Saviour, or I die.[14]

He had nothing in his hand (only nails through his wrists); he was naked on the cross, he was helpless and he was stained by his sin. And yet—here is Jesus saying *Yes* to him. There is a place for any sinner who comes to Christ in repentance and faith.

Truly this man *does* receive sinners. The Pharisees and scribes meant it as an accusation, but it is good news, the gospel according to Christ's enemies.

[14] Hymn, 'Rock of Ages' by Augustus Montague Toplady (1740–78).

Matchless Words

Speeches that Changed the World is the title of a book[1] that highlights the words of many famous people and illustrates the power of words to make a difference. It includes such famous orations as Martin Luther King's 'I have a dream' speech, the Gettysburg Address and some of the inspiring words that rallied the British people during the Second World War ('Never in the field of human conflict was so much owed by so many to so few', etc).

Interestingly, the first speech included in the book is the Decalogue (the Ten Commandments), as recorded in Exodus 20, and the second is the Sermon on the Mount from chapters five to seven of Matthew's gospel. Matthew records the words of Jesus and then tells of their impact: 'When Jesus finished these sayings, the crowds were astonished at his teaching, for he was teaching them as one who had authority, and not as their scribes' (Matt. 7:28, 29). That highlights the effect of Jesus' words on those who heard them, and on that occasion came from people who were presumably sympathetic rather than antipathetic to him.

But there is another occasion when we hear something similar from people who were enemies of Christ—words which were

---

[1] *Speeches that Changed the World* (London: Quercus Publishing Ltd, 2005).

intended as an attack but which were unintentionally true. The words are those of John 7:46: 'No one ever spoke like this man.'

There is *the gospel according to Christ's enemies.*

Whatever was in their minds when they spoke the words, they spoke the truth and the words of Jesus Christ have stood ever since in their peerless power and their matchless message.

They have even found their way into common language and many people use his words without realising that they are doing so. The English language is full of biblical expressions and, from the words of Jesus in the gospels, people will talk about turning the other cheek, being of good cheer, putting their hand to the plough, being a good Samaritan, the blind leading the blind, being the salt of the earth—and there are many other expressions that people use without realising or remembering their source.[2]

But it's more than just the enrichment of the language! The words of Jesus have reverberated around the world ever since they were spoken two millennia ago; truly 'No one ever spoke like this man.'

Opposition to Jesus on the part of the Jewish religious establishment had been growing. There was much public discussion about what was going on and Matthew tells us that when they 'heard the crowd muttering these things,' the chief priests and Pharisees sent officers to arrest him. It was the time of the Feast of Tabernacles, one of the high points of the year for Jewish people, and Jesus had been attracting much attention with his—as these officers came to realise—unique teaching.

John's account says: 'The officers then came to the chief priests and Pharisees, who said to them, "Why did you not bring him?"' We might imagine the officers looking down at their feet in

[2] Many of such expressions come, in particular, from the 1611 Authorised (or King James) Version of the Bible, and the examples given come from: Matt. 5:39, John 16:33, Luke 9:62, Luke 10:33, Luke 6:39 and Matt. 5:13.

embarrassment as they answered, 'No one ever spoke like this man.' The Pharisees challenged them, 'Have you also been deceived? Have any of the authorities or the Pharisees believed in him?' (John 7:45-48).

So it is that we have gospel truth expressed by the enemies of Christ. The officers themselves might have said that they weren't actual enemies of Jesus—they were only trying to earn their daily denarius. But with these words they sought to excuse their empty-handed return—no Jesus with hands tied behind his back. Perhaps they also meant that they themselves had been impressed by what they heard from Jesus' lips.

However, they were the servants of the Pharisees and priests who decidedly *were* Jesus' enemies and we can take these words, like others highlighted in this book, to be expressive of the gospel according to the enemies of Christ.

A note of authority

What was it that impressed these temple police officers? For one thing, there was the authority with which Jesus spoke. We know from Matthew 7:29 that this was something which struck Jesus' hearers. They were used to hearing religious leaders speaking tentatively, often simply quoting the words of this or that rabbi, whereas Jesus' words had the ring of personal, underived authority about them.

The gospels constantly record his teaching beginning with words such as 'Truly I say to you...' (for example, Matt. 8:10; 11:11; the Authorised Version's famous 'Verily') and the Sermon on the Mount includes six occasions in which Jesus would refer to what others had said and then go on, 'But *I* say to you...' He didn't need to quote other teachers or hide behind their reputations, much less ride on the coat-tails of famous orators.

We are told that he taught with authority. That didn't mean that he spoke with a loud voice (like the politician who wrote in the margin of his notes for a speech, 'Argument weak here—shout louder'). It was simply that he spoke with an authority that commanded attention. There was something compelling and winsome about his words, an authority that came from the uniqueness of his nature as the Son of God.

Many other speeches have made a difference and have been long remembered, but 'no one ever spoke like this man' whose words will outlast all others. He himself said, 'Heaven and earth will pass away, but my words will not pass away' (Matt. 24:35).

Many have predicted that his words and influence would pass away—people like the cynical Voltaire who proclaimed that he was tired of hearing it said that it only took twelve men to set up Christianity, and he would show that it would only take one man to destroy it. Actually Christianity *wasn't* set up by the twelve disciples but by Jesus himself, but such were the words of Voltaire; yet few today remember Voltaire, while Jesus is honoured by millions.

Heinrich Himmler, one of Hitler's generals, prophesied during the Second World War that the Führer would replace Christ as the saviour of humanity; he said, 'Millions and millions of people will say only Hitler's name in their prayers and, a hundred years from now, nothing will be known but the new religion'.[3]

But, as the evening hymn says, 'So be it, Lord! Thy throne shall never, like earth's proud empires, pass away; Thy Kingdom stands and grows for ever.'[4]

These enemies of Christ (or employees of his enemies) said more than they realised in their report, 'No one ever spoke like this man.'

[3] Quoted by Derick Bingham in an article in *Christian Herald*, 24 June 1995.
[4] Hymn, 'The Day Thou gavest' by John Ellerton, 1826–93.

So far we have been referring to the *manner* of his speaking—with authority—but what about the *content* of his teaching?

What he said about God

For one thing, no one ever spoke like this man about God.

Perhaps this is the thing that struck these temple guards, so that we could imagine a conversation as they made their way back empty-handed:

A—*There's something about that man, isn't there?*

B—*Yes, his words were ordinary Aramaic words, but I've never heard anyone speak like him.*

A—*Did you hear how he spoke about God? I've always believed that there is a God, but to me he's a distant power. He spoke of him as a Father who is near.*

B—*How could we arrest the speaker of such amazing words?*

And when they did report back and make their declaration, we are told that they were derided by the Pharisees for their naivety: *Don't tell us you've been taken in as well. Don't you realise that none of the people who matter has a good word to say about him—it's just the rabble of common folk who don't know any better. They've been moved by the emotion, swayed by fine rhetoric, captivated by someone upon whom they could pin their hopes of freedom and deliverance.*

After all, they might have added, *he comes from Galilee and everybody knows prophets don't come from Galilee; if God wanted to send a special messenger, he'd obviously send him here to Jerusalem to be born and brought up, wouldn't he?*

The end of John 7 tells us that this was in fact the way they spoke to one of their number who posed the question, 'Does our law judge a man without first giving him a hearing and learning what he does?' The man's name was Nicodemus and he must have been walking a tight-rope, since he was a secret follower of Jesus—John 3 tells of his clandestine visit one night to converse with Jesus.

In the present situation he was prepared to speak up for fair play. He was indeed 'one of their number' (a Pharisee) but he was not in sympathy with their attitude to Jesus. Maybe he too realised that no one ever spoke as Jesus spoke. He could surely remember Jesus' words about the need to be born again and about God loving the world so much that he sent his only Son into the world, that whoever believes in him should not perish but have everlasting life (John 3:16).

No one spoke as Jesus spoke about God. Others may have referred to the almightiness of God but often he was regarded as a distant Being; some would have referred to him as the Judge of the world, more a Power to be feared than a Father to be loved. And, although Jesus had plenty to say about judgement to come, he also spoke of God as a loving Father. Wasn't that indeed the theme of that famous parable—the loving Father who longed for his wayward sons to come home? (Luke 15:11-32). Most strikingly of all, he would say things like, 'Whoever has seen me has seen the Father' (John 14:9) and 'I and the Father are one' (John 10:30).

So much for the idea that Jesus was a purveyor of nice thoughts about a distant deity or the notion that he just had some new and interesting insights. His words were striking indeed and they faced people with a choice. People could conclude that he was a deluded fanatic who had gotten too much 'religion' for his own good; they could dismiss him as a harmless fraud. But they couldn't come away with talk about him being a good teacher and example. Either his words were sober truth and he was one with the Father or he was dangerously deluded and needed to be locked up for his own good!

No one ever spoke like this man—about God.

What he said about human beings

Secondly, there is what he said about people. His words and his actions show that he did not treat any individuals or groups as useless or unimportant, nor did he show favouritism to anyone. He did not regard anyone as beyond redemption, but neither did he go along with the notion that human beings are basically quite nice and just need a little encouragement to live decent lives.

It is true that the teaching of Jesus gives great dignity and significance to human beings, viewing them as creatures made in the image of God. He said, 'Are not two sparrows sold for a penny? And not one of them will fall to the ground apart from your Father. But even the hairs of your head are all numbered. Fear not, therefore; you are of more value than many sparrows' (Matt. 10:29-31).

In one sense we human beings may seem *in*significant. As one astrophysicist has written, '…we're really highly insignificant in the grand scheme of things—just one out of seven billion people on planet Earth, orbiting just one star out of 100 billion stars in our Milky Way galaxy, just one galaxy out of 100 billion galaxies in our observable universe.'[5]

Yet the Bible's message is that each human being is significant. We are not the products of impersonal chance or evolution. We are made in God's image and, as one evangelist has written, 'Jesus set a high value on persons *because* they were made by a personal

---

[5] Professor Catherine Heymans in 2019 Edinburgh University magazine, *Edit*, 29.

God; the atheist professes high regard for persons *despite* the fact that they are products of a quite impassive and impersonal universe. That is the irreconcilable difference between the Christian and the atheistic position.'[6]

It is striking that John's gospel, in consecutive chapters, tells of Jesus interacting with very different people. In chapter 3 he spent time with Nicodemus who was 'a ruler of the Jews', a member of the Sanhedrin who would have been influential and probably also wealthy, and then, in chapter 4, he interacted with the unnamed woman of Samaria who seems to have been a social outcast because of her scandalous lifestyle (five marriages in her past and unmarried cohabitation in her present). She would have been ostracised by many people, but Jesus took time to converse with her and point her to the living water that could quench her inner thirst for solidity and meaning in her life.

This illustrates Jesus' regard for human beings as individuals. On another occasion he spoke about God as the Giver of life (Matt. 19:4). He also said then that 'from the beginning God made them male and female.' Within a few verses he taught important principles. He talked about 'the beginning'—our world and the universe are not eternal; they had a beginning. Genesis says it: 'In the beginning God created the heavens and the earth' (Gen. 1:1). Mankind also had a beginning.

In Matthew 19 Jesus referred to that beginning. He was answering some Pharisees who were trying to trick him with a question about divorce, and in response he referred them back to God's creation plan: 'Have you not read that he who created them from the beginning made them male and female, and said, "Therefore a man shall leave his father and his mother and hold fast to his wife, and the two shall become one flesh. So they are

---

[6] Michael Green, *Runaway World* (London: IVP, 1968), 52.

no longer two but one flesh. What therefore God has joined together, let not man separate"' (Matt. 19:4-6).

We learn from the Lord's matchless words about human beings that marriage—the life-long, exclusive union of a man and a woman—can never be regarded as unimportant or outmoded. It is part of God's plan for human life. For some people his plan is that they should remain single (he himself did not marry), but he emphasises that marriage and family are part of the divine plan for human life. Both individuals and society suffer when this is neglected or opposed.

His enemies said, 'No one ever spoke like this man' and his words have elevated the position of mankind and the value of the individual through the centuries.

Yet at the same time Jesus' words were also intensely realistic. In the Sermon on the Mount, he uttered one little phrase which reveals much. Talking about God's desire to enrich life, he said 'If you then, who are evil, know how to give good gifts to your children, how much more will your Father who is in heaven give good things to those who ask him!' (Matt. 7:11). That phrase 'who are evil' gives the lie to any idealised picture of human beings, and testifies to all that the Bible says about human beings as being fallen. He also said, 'Out of the heart come evil thoughts, murder, adultery, sexual immorality, theft, false witness, slander' (Matt. 15:19), and in John 3:19 he spoke about people loving 'the darkness rather than the light because their works were evil.'

Such was the realism of Jesus' teaching, that teaching which so impressed the soldiers who were sent to arrest him.

Paul would later write, 'All have sinned' (past tense) 'and fall short' (present tense) of the glory of God, words which may have been in the mind of Aleksandr Solzhenitsyn when he wrote, 'If only there were some evil people somewhere, insidiously committing evil deeds, and it were necessary only to separate them off from the rest of us. But the line dividing good and evil cuts through every human heart.'[7]

No one spoke about such matters like Jesus, and if his words about our fallenness are stark and straightforward, so are his words about the danger of condemnation because of our sinfulness. In the sermon in which he referred to the Father's provision for the birds of the air and added, 'Are you not of more value than they?' He also spoke about the dreadful declaration on judgement day, 'I never knew you; depart from me' (Matt. 6:26; 7:23). He even said, 'Do not fear those who can kill the body but cannot kill the soul. Rather fear him who can destroy both soul and body in hell' (Matt. 10:28).

As will be pointed out later (chapter 11), Jesus spoke much about judgement and hell. He did so not because he exulted in it, but because it is vital that people should face up to it.

No one spoke like this man about human beings.

What he said about salvation

We can also say—no one ever spoke like him about salvation. We are told that on the last day of the Feast of Tabernacles, Jesus stood in the temple grounds and said, 'If anyone thirsts, let him come to me and drink. Whoever believes in me, as the Scripture has said, "Out of his heart will flow rivers of living water."' (John 7:37, 38).

That is the immediate context in which the Temple officers' words are recorded. John does not specifically say that these were the words they heard, but presumably by recording things in this

---

[7] Aleksandr Solzhenitsyn, *The Gulag Archipelago* (New York: Harper & Row, 1973), 615-17.

order he means us to understand that this is what left them confused and perhaps mesmerised.

Several times in the gospels we find this image: Jesus is the One who can quench the thirst of the human soul. Thirst for what? It is the thirst for ultimate satisfaction in life, for an assurance that our sins are forgiven, a sense that there is meaning to life and a message about what lies beyond the horizon that we call death.

It is the image behind Horatius Bonar's hymn, in which each verse has a first half about the invitation of Christ and a second half which is the testimony of the believer. One verse says:

> I heard the voice of Jesus say, 'Behold I freely give
>   The living water; thirsty one, stoop down and drink and live.'
> I came to Jesus and I drank of that life-giving stream;
>   My thirst was quenched, my soul revived and now
>   I live in Him.[8]

Other teachers and other systems of thought may tell people what they have to *do* to be saved—what a good life they must live, how many good deeds they must perform, what standard they have to reach—but no one spoke like Jesus when he said things like, 'Come to me and drink' (John 7:37), 'No one comes to the Father except through me' (John 14:6) and 'I stand at the door and knock; if anyone hears my voice and opens the door, I will come in to him' (Rev. 3:20).

There is in the human heart a thirst for something to give meaning and significance to life; observation and experience confirm that *things* can't deliver the goods. People can have huge amounts of money and possessions; they can have fame, success and popularity—and still be empty and unfulfilled.

[8] Hymn by Horatius Bonar (1808–89).

Even the famous polymath Bertrand Russell said, 'The centre of me is always and eternally... searching for something beyond what the world contains'[9] and a recent book by two psychiatrists says, 'Hopelessness permeates the lives of our contemporaries. The actor Marlon Brando reflected this spirit well: "Life is a mystery and it is an unsolvable one. You just simply live it through and as you draw your last breath you say, What was that all about?"'[10]

And what if there is an even deeper problem, connected with our sin and imperfection? If God is holy and perfect and we are not, what hope can there ever be of our being in the right with him? If there is a gulf between us and God, how can that gulf ever be crossed?

This is the ultimate question. Many try to excuse, explain away or re-define our sinfulness, but it remains the case that none of us will claim to be what we know we should be.

We need something to be done about our sin, and no one spoke like Jesus about what he had come to do. He spoke of his own death as a sacrifice for sin, as a means of taking our sin upon himself and undergoing the righteous wrath of Almighty God in our place. He said he had come not to be served but to serve and to give his life as a ransom for many (Mark 10:45).

He said to little Zacchaeus (to take one example), 'Today salvation has come to this house' (Luke 19:9). This was said immediately after Zacchaeus vowed to give half of his goods to the poor and restore fourfold anything that he had taken from others by fraud, but it was not Zacchaeus' action that earned his salvation. It was the action that *showed* his salvation. People were grumbling about Jesus having the time of day for someone who was

---

[9] *Autobiography* (London: George Allen & Unwin, 1967), 303.
[10] Pablo Martinez & Andrew Sims, *Mad or God?* (London: IVP, 2018), 150.

obviously a sinner, but Zacchaeus showed by his response that he had received the forgiveness and salvation of Jesus.

In the eighteenth century there was a Christian lady with the title Countess of Huntingdon. She had a desire to share the gospel with people in her upper-class circles and invited one such, the Dowager Duchess of Buckingham, to a meeting at which George Whitefield was to preach.

The Duchess's reply was:

> I thank your ladyship for the information concerning the Methodist preachers. Their doctrines are most repulsive and strongly tinctured with impertinence and disrespect before their superiors, in perpetually endeavouring to level all ranks and do away with all distinctions. It is monstrous to be told you have a heart as sinful as the common wretches that crawl on the earth. This is highly offensive.[11]

I don't think she wanted to go! Of course, that attitude has to be seen against the background of the class-ridden society that Great Britain then was, but she spoke of the preachers 'doing away with all distinctions.' Actually, it is God who does that; Romans 3:22 says, 'There is no distinction for all have sinned and fall short of the glory of God.' And it goes on: '...and are justified freely by his grace through the redemption that came by Christ Jesus.'

That is the way of salvation, and it is the way of salvation for all classes and conditions of human beings. It is the truth expressed in the old hymn:

> What can wash away my sin?
>   Nothing but the blood of Jesus.
> What can make me whole again?
>   Nothing but the blood of Jesus.
> Nothing can for sin atone—

[11] Quoted by Mark Meynell, *Cross-Examined* (Leicester: IVP, 2001), 36.

The Gospel According to Christ's Enemies

> nothing but the blood of Jesus,
> Naught of good that I have done—
> nothing but the blood of Jesus.[12]

No one spoke like Jesus about salvation.

What he said about morality

Also, no one spoke like this Man about morality. One of his principal controversies with the religious leaders of the day was over the externals of religion, because it seems that so many people thought that the formal performance of certain rituals and ceremonies would put them right in God's sight.

In Matthew 23 we find some of the sternest words Jesus spoke, and they were addressed to the religious leaders of the day. He spoke of them tithing even the herbs of their fields but neglecting the weightier matters—justice, mercy and faithfulness. He said, 'Woe to you, scribes and Pharisees, hypocrites! For you clean the outside of the cup and the plate, but inside they are full of greed and self-indulgence' and even, 'You are like whitewashed tombs, which outwardly appear beautiful, but within are full of dead people's bones and all uncleanness. So you also outwardly appear righteous to others, but within you are full of hypocrisy and lawlessness' (Matt. 23:23-28).

No one had spoken to them like that before!

And no one spoke in the way that Jesus spoke in the Sermon on the Mount where, six times, we find a formulaic statement, 'You have heard that it was said... But I say to you' (Matt. 5:21-48).

He pressed matters from the outward action to the inner motivation of the heart, as, for example, with the commandment not

---

[12] Hymn by Robert Lowry (1826–99).

to commit murder. This was one of the basic commandments, but what *he* said was, 'But I say to you that everyone who is angry with his brother will be liable to judgement' (Matt 5:22). Similarly with the commandment prohibiting adultery, he said, 'But I say to you that everyone who looks at a woman with lustful intent has already committed adultery with her in his heart' (Matt 5:28).

The other subjects concern divorce, oaths, and revenge, and the series culminates in the words, 'You have heard that it was said, "You shall love your neighbour and hate your enemy."' As we saw earlier, that had *not* been said in the Old Testament; Jesus was correcting a misinterpretation of the law. He said, 'But I say to you, Love your enemies and pray for those who persecute you... If you love only those who love you, what reward do you have?' (Matt 5:43-48).

No one spoke like this Man about morality. Far from lessening God's demands, his concern was to get behind outward actions to the inner motivation of the heart. And it was this searching nature of his teaching that led to the statement at the end of the Sermon on the Mount that he taught as One who had authority (Matt 7:29).

Again, the charge, 'No one spoke like this man', expressed by his enemies, was remarkably true.

What he said about contentment

Also, no one spoke like him about peace and contentment. Stress is regarded by some people as a feature of modern life, and perhaps there are particular stresses attached to life in this age of political confusion, economic uncertainty and digital bombard-ment. But people have always lived under stresses of one kind or another. And at the end of Matthew 11 we find Jesus saying,

'Come to me, all who labour and are heavy laden, and I will give you rest' (Matt. 11:28). Here too are words of which it can be said, 'No one ever spoke like this man.'

Others may offer their recipes for the way to peace and contentment, and even their techniques for attaining inner tranquillity; Jesus says, 'Come to me'—not to a technique, a mantra, or a list of steps towards inner peace; simply, 'Come to me.'

It is a huge claim, and it is the heart of the gospel, for it is through his forgiveness and salvation that the barriers to inner peace are removed. And it is faith in him that leads to that great blessing.

That is stated elsewhere in Scripture: 'You keep him in perfect peace whose mind is stayed on you, because he trusts in you' (Isa. 26:3). That is not about an airy-fairy or other-worldly peace, as if Christianity were a religion that denies all the hard knocks of this life and pretends that life can be lived on a perpetual high. The faith of the Bible is grounded in this world with all its troubles, trials and tragedies. Christ's words do not lead us to pretend that such burdens are illusory. He says rather, 'I will give you rest. Take my yoke upon you, and learn from me, for I am gentle and lowly in heart, and you will find rest for your souls.' The image no doubt comes from the yokes Jesus would have made in the carpenter's shop at Nazareth and it suggests the image of Jesus on one side of the yoke and the believer on the other, going along in tandem.

What he said about values

No one ever spoke like Jesus about God, about salvation, about morality, about peace—or about values. Some of his sayings show the way in which he was turning the world upside-down.

For example, he said, 'Whoever would be great among you must be your servant, and whoever would be first among you must be slave of all' (Mark 10:43, 44), and 'If anyone would come after me, let him deny himself and take up his cross and follow me. For whoever would save his life will lose it, but whoever loses his life for my sake and the gospel's will save it. For what does it profit a man to gain the whole world and forfeit his soul?' (Mark 8:34-37).

So it is that Jesus turns the values of the world upside-down. God's way is the way of self-sacrifice, not self-promotion; it is the way of spending one's self, not the way of pleasing one's self. It is the way of love.

One of his famous parables was told to illustrate his theme that 'One's life does not consist in the abundance of his possessions':

> The land of a rich man produced plentifully, and he thought to himself, 'What shall I do, for I have nowhere to store my crops?' And he said, 'I will do this: I will tear down my barns and build bigger ones, and there I will store all my grain and my goods. And I will say to my soul, "Soul, you have ample goods laid up for many years; relax, eat, drink and be merry." But God said to him, 'Fool! This night your soul is required of you, and the things you have prepared, whose will they be?' So is the one who lays up treasure for himself and is not rich towards God" (Luke 12:13-21).

It's all about priorities. Jesus wasn't saying that the farmer was wrong to be successful and prosperous. The man's mistake was not in being wealthy but in making wealth the most important thing in his life.

There is a story about two people walking along a busy street in New York City. One of them was a native American and in the midst of all the noise and bustle he stopped and said, 'Listen. I can hear a cricket.' His companion was incredulous; how could he possibly hear a cricket amid all the noise around them?

But his friend insisted and eventually tracked the sound down to a waste bin. He rummaged about with his hand until, sure enough, he found the cricket. His friend was amazed and said, 'You must have the most amazing ears.' The native American replied, 'No, I have ears like everybody else's, but my ears are attuned to that kind of sound.'

To demonstrate his meaning, he took from his pocket a handful of loose change and threw the coins into the air so that they clattered down on to the pavement/sidewalk. Despite all the traffic noise, people for two blocks stopped and looked round! They recognised *that* sound; their ears were attuned to the sound of money.

The story illustrates what Jesus said about values. The most important things in life are not 'things' at all. Solomon was probably one of the richest men of his time but his testimony is salutary; this is from the second chapter of Ecclesiastes:

> I made great works. I built houses and planted vineyards for myself. I made myself gardens and parks, and planted in them all kinds of fruit trees. I made myself pools from which to water the forest of growing trees. I bought male and female slaves, and had slaves who were born in my house. I had also great possessions of herds and flocks, more than any who had been before me in Jerusalem. I also gathered for myself silver and gold and the treasure of kings and provinces. I got singers, both men and women, and many concubines, the delight of the sons of man (Eccles. 2:4).

Such was his success, but after it all he wrote, 'Then I considered all that my hands had done and the toil I had expended in doing it, and behold, all was vanity and a striving after wind, and there was nothing to be gained under the sun' (Eccl. 2:11).

The whole theme of *Ecclesiastes* is that our principal need is to be rightly related to God. It is 'the fear of the Lord' that is the beginning of wisdom (Prov. 9:10)—not *beginning* as something that can be cast aside once it has been mastered, but *beginning* in the sense in which learning your scales is the beginning and abiding foundation of musical accomplishment. That knowledge underlies everything that follows in the playing of great music, and the fear of the Lord is the underlying factor that informs everything about the life of faith.

The *fear of God,* in this context, means a proper attitude of faith and trust. Scripture calls us to turn from our sin and self-centredness and put our trust in the One who 'suffered once for sins, the righteous for the unrighteous, that he might bring us to God' (1 Pet. 3:18).

His enemies said, 'No one ever spoke like this man.' How right they were! His words are incomparable—about God, about human beings, about salvation, about morality, about contentment, about values. They are unique words from a unique Person; the gospel—according to Christ's enemies.

4

In the National Interest

One of the most striking examples of irony in the New Testament is found in John 11:50 where we are privy to a meeting of the Sanhedrin, the Jewish Council.

The members of the Council had heard reports about Jesus raising a dead man back to life—and they realised they'd have to do something. Part of their concern was that, if Jesus' popularity continued to grow, a volatile situation might arise which could lead to a violent intervention by the Romans who had the upper hand at the time.

And so it was that Caiaphas, the Jewish High Priest at the time, spoke up. The apostle John must have had some inside information, and he gives a snatch of the discussion. Caiaphas said to the others, 'You know nothing at all,' (John 11:49), which was pretty dismissive, tantamount to calling them ignorant fools. He went on, 'Nor do you understand that it is better for you that one man should die for the people, not that the whole nation should perish' (John 11:50).

John then goes on to draw attention to the unintended significance of Caiaphas' words: 'He did not say this of his own accord, but being high priest that year he prophesied that Jesus would die for the nation, and not for the nation only, but also to gather into one the children of God who are scattered abroad.' (*The Message*[1] paraphrases it, 'He unwittingly prophesied that Jesus was about to die sacrificially for the nation, and not only for the nation…').

From that time on, John tells us, they made plans to get Jesus put to death (verses 51-53).

The voice of Caiaphas is that of the cynical manipulator; he saw Jesus as a threat—not only to the nation but also to his own position and power. So, posing as a patriot who was acting for national security, he advocated the unfortunate sacrifice of this one Man in order to prevent dire consequences for the nation as a whole. Not for him such considerations as what would be the *right* thing to do; all he cared about was expediency. Caiaphas is the forerunner of all who place expediency above principle, who are more concerned with their own advantage than with right and wrong.

Obviously he had no intention of saying anything prophetic about Jesus' *yielding of his life as an atonement for sin,*[2] but his words did in fact point to something he did not mean to say.

The Bible's teaching *is* that one Man died for the people; his death *was* a sacrificial death, a substitutionary death, a death by which others may enter into life.

It is just what was expressed in the famous gospel verse found a few chapters earlier—John 3:16: 'God so loved the world that he gave his one and only Son, that whoever believes in him shall not perish but have eternal life.' It goes on, 'For God did not send his Son into the world to condemn the world, but to save the world through him.'

The phrase in the Apostles' Creed, 'suffered under Pontius Pilate, was crucified, dead and buried,' is not only the description

[1] Eugene Peterson, *The Message* (Colorado Springs: NavPress, 1993).
[2] Lines from hymn, 'To God be the Glory' by Fanny Crosby (1820–1915).

of a monumental miscarriage of justice, nor is it simply an example of fortitude in the face of unjust treatment. It is all of that, but it is so much more. It is all about God's remedy for sin. That 'one man' did die so that others should not perish, and it is through him that there is good news of deliverance and salvation.

'The cross', it has been said in a fine expression, 'is the only place where the loving, forgiving, merciful God is revealed in such a way that we perceive that his holiness and his love are equally infinite.'[3] It speaks of the holiness of One who cannot look upon sin—his holiness is infinite. So is his love, the love that drew salvation's plan, fashioning a way of salvation for all who will receive it, a way in which we see that God is, as Paul wrote, both just and the justifier of those who put their faith in Jesus (Rom. 3:26). The cross is the place where the Son of God took on our sin and died in our place.

All human illustrations have their limitations, but they can throw some light on the matter—stories like that of Maximilian Kolbe, a Polish priest who was imprisoned in Auschwitz in 1941.

A prisoner had managed to escape, and in reprisal the Nazis decided that ten prisoners were to die—by starvation. One of the ten—prisoner 5,659—was a family man called Franciscek Gajowniczek, and Kolbe, prisoner 16,670, volunteered to take his place. He was kept in a starvation bunker for two weeks and then given a lethal injection of carbolic acid.

Thirty years later, a survivor wrote:

> It was an enormous shock to the whole camp. We became aware that one among us in the spiritual dark night of the soul was raising the standard of love on high. Someone unknown, like everyone else, tortured and bereft of name and social

[3] Emil Brunner, *The Mediator* (Cambridge: Lutterworth Press, 1934), 470.

standing, went to a horrible death for the sake of someone not even related to him.[4]

Kolbe's action was an amazing act of courage and self-sacrifice; he gave his own life so that the other might live. It is clearly a story of tremendous human heroism. It is also a picture of the message of the cross, where one Man—the truly innocent Man—gave himself up to death in order that others might be delivered.

Caiaphas' words (little did he realise it) give us the gospel according to Christ's enemies. What would he have thought if he had known that his words would be quoted down through the centuries, albeit with a different meaning from his intention?

Caiaphas was concerned about a dreaded possibility—political disaster—but there is something much worse than that: the dreadful possibility of (as 1 Cor. 15:17 puts it) being 'still in our sins.' Faith enables us to sing:

> He took my sins and my sorrows;
> He made them His very own;
> He bore the burden to Calvary
> And suffered and died alone.
> How marvellous, how wonderful
> Is my Saviour's love for me. [5]

As mentioned above, this meeting of the Sanhedrin was called in the aftermath of the raising of Lazarus, that most astonishing of all the astonishing miracles of Jesus. John seems to go to lengths to demonstrate that there was no trickery, even to the extent of letting us overhear Martha's practical objection to Jesus' command to open the tomb. She said, 'Lord, by this time there will be an odour, for he has been dead four days' (John 11:39).

---

[4] https://willvaus.blogspot.com/2018/06/why-did-jesus-die-on-cross.html (accessed 11 May 2019).

[5] Hymn, 'I Stand Amazed' by Charles Hutchinson Gabriel (1858–1932).

And when it happened, when Lazarus came forth and was later seen walking around—very much alive—and when many of the (as the leaders would have said, simple-minded and easily-deluded) people believed in Jesus, and others reported it to the chief priests and Pharisees, they realised that they had a problem on their hands.

'What are we to do?' they asked each other. They couldn't actually deny that Lazarus was alive, and it was very hard to argue that he had never really been dead, and so we overhear them saying to each other, 'This man (Jesus) performs many signs. If we let him go on like this, everyone will believe in him'—and if that's bad, what is even worse is, 'the Romans will come and take away both our place and our nation' (John 11:48). The place would be the temple, and the nation, which was already under Roman administration and domination, would be ground into the dust.

Expediency or principle?

It is in the midst of this debate that we are given the opportunity to hear what Caiaphas said. He had been appointed in AD 18 by Pontius Pilate's predecessor; by this time, about eleven years later, Caiaphas had established himself and he certainly didn't want his position and power to be threatened.

Although Palestine was occupied territory, Rome was reasonably tolerant. Indeed, Roman rule brought some advantages to subjugated lands, notably the famous *pax Romana* and *lex Romana*—Roman peace and Roman law. But everyone knew that Rome was ruthless in its response to any revolution, or even threat of it.

It had happened before. Luke's gospel refers to a man called Barabbas who was eventually released when Pilate offered the

Passover amnesty and the people could choose either Jesus or Barabbas. There were enough agitators to whip up support for Barabbas. We don't know much about him, but Luke 23:19 describes him as 'a man who had been thrown into prison for an insurrection started in the city and for murder,' and in those days prison was not the punishment but the place where you awaited your punishment. He was awaiting crucifixion, the no-nonsense way in which Rome dealt with rebels.

There had been many attempted rebellions—and there had been many crucifixions. Caiaphas' calculation was that it would be worth one more if it would save the nation—and preserve his own position: It may be regrettable, folks, but politics is politics!

There *were* people who saw Jesus as a champion who might lead a revolution against Rome. Much of what Jesus said and did, as recorded in the four gospels, has to be seen against that background. But he repudiated that idea—not because politics is unimportant, but because he had come for a higher purpose. We know that Jesus never had any plans to initiate an armed uprising, but Caiaphas and the others felt threatened and, as the King James Version puts it, he came right out with it—insulting the others as clueless and then saying 'It is expedient for us, that one man should die for the people, and that the whole nation perish not.'

Unintended truth

Unwittingly, Caiaphas gave expression to the gospel message. There is a kind of double irony in his words, because in the first place the exact opposite of what he desired actually happened. After the crucifixion, it was only a few decades before the Romans did come to 'take away both our place and our nation.' Caiaphas thought he had succeeded in getting rid of Jesus in the name of national security (how frustrated he must have been when rumours of the resurrection were circulating), but the national security he prized was short lived.

However, there's a greater irony in the other way in which his words were true.

When I was a child, if people unintentionally spoke some words that rhymed, they might say, 'I'm a poet and I didn't know it.' Caiaphas was a prophet and didn't know it—that doesn't rhyme but it fits the facts. He obviously did not intend to prophesy anything about the meaning of Jesus' death, but that is what happened. His words meant something that he never intended. 'He prophesied that Jesus would die for the nation;' (John 11:51) that is the gospel according to this enemy of Christ.

He spoke about preventing the nation perishing. It is the very word used earlier in the most well-known verse in John's gospel: 'God so loved the world, that he gave his only Son, that whoever believes in him should *not perish* but have eternal life' (John 3:16). The implication is obviously that without such faith in Christ people will perish.

It is in many ways an unpalatable teaching, but it is the truth according to the Bible—without this salvation, people are heading for a Christless eternity. It is a dreadful thought, and whether it is palatable or not is not the point.

Imagine you had a great aunt you'd never heard of in Australia who has written to you. You've conversed by telephone and you have built up a picture of what you think she looks like. Then you have the chance to visit Australia and she's there to meet you at the airport—only, she turns out to look completely different from your image. You thought she'd be tall and dark and she turns out to be little and auburn. Which picture of your aunt are you going to accept—the picture you had, or the reality in front of you?

In relation to ultimate issues, are we to imagine what *we* think God and his truth are like, or are we to accept and respond to what he has actually made known to us? It is one of the tragedies of our age that so many (sometimes even within the professing church) think we know better than God, so that we can fashion our own theories and theology, and many choose to ignore altogether the things revealed about the judgement that awaits us all when this life is over.

J. B. Phillips wrote, 'Jesus was no sentimental do-gooder and he spoke quite unequivocally about rewards and punishments in the world to come.' He pointed out that some of the most terrifying words in the New Testament come from the mouth of none other than Jesus himself—'Yet they are not threats or menaces but warnings given in deadly earnest by the incarnation of unsentimental love.'[6]

We easily understand that there is a difference between a threat and a warning. A threat is normally given in malice, but a warning is given in love and concern that some undesirable outcome should be avoided.

Caiaphas and John agree about the dreadful possibility of perishing but, of course, the messages are quite different, and when John 3:16 speaks about perishing, it is expressing the gospel message that wants people not to perish but to have eternal life.

The glory of the cross

Caiaphas unwittingly expressed the truth when he spoke about

---

[6] *Ring of Truth—A Translator's Testimony* (London: Hodder & Stoughton, 1967), 68.

Jesus dying so that others should not perish. That is the message of the gospel; it is the glory of the cross.

Such a message might have been expected to be an unwelcome embarrassment to the church. After all, a cross was a symbol of shameful and torturous defeat and death. Yet the early Church gloried in it, and generations of Christians have sung words which would have seemed bizarre to most people in that first century world:

> In the cross of Christ I glory,
> Towering o'er the wrecks of time;
> All the light of sacred story
> Gathers round its head sublime.[7]

Far from being an embarrassment to Christians, the cross was and is the symbol of God's great salvation.

Paul referred to it as a stumbling-block to Jews (1 Cor. 1:23). He probably had in mind the words of Deuteronomy 21:23, 'A hanged man is cursed by God.' So the Jews might say, 'How could anyone who was nailed to a cross be God's Son or the Messiah?' It didn't occur to them, even with Isaiah 53 in their hands (about the suffering servant who would be bruised for others' iniquities) that this could actually be God's way, that that very verse about a crucified person being cursed might be answered by Galatians 3:13 where Paul wrote, 'Christ redeemed us from the curse of the law by becoming a curse for us, for it is written, "Cursed is everyone who is hung in a tree"'(Gal. 3:13).

Another reason why the message of the cross might have been a stumbling-block to Jews was the expectation that the Messiah, when he came, would perform spectacular signs. 1 Corinthians 1:22 says as much: 'Jews demand signs.' Jesus, however,

---

[7] Hymn, *In the cross of Christ I glory*, by John Bowring (1792–1872).

deliberately turned away from the performance of spectacular deeds to 'prove himself.' The gospels tell of people coming and asking for a sign from heaven, but he steadfastly refused to fit into that mould of miracle-working sensationalist. Yet there were miracles, and the raising of Lazarus was one of the most amazing—and troublesome for some.

Paul wrote, 'Jews demand signs and Greeks seek wisdom, but we preach Christ crucified, a stumbling block to Jews and folly to Gentiles, but to those who are called, both Jews and Greeks, Christ the power of God and the wisdom of God' (1 Cor. 1:22-24).

That stratagem of God (if we can so call it) is seen in the composition of his church as well as in this central message of the cross.

So far as the church is concerned, verse 26 says, 'Not many of you were wise according to worldly standards, not many were powerful, not many were of noble birth. But God chose what is foolish in the world to shame the wise; God chose what is weak in the world to shame the strong.'

In the second century there was a Greek philosopher called Celsus who wrote what has been described as the earliest known comprehensive criticism of Christianity (although Celsus' writing is only known through words of it that Origen quotes in his *Contra Celsum*). He said that the very fact that Christians regard the lowest of people as worthy of their God showed that they wanted, and were able to convince, only foolish, dishonourable and stupid people—slaves, women and little children.

One could never get away with such language today, but that was the attitude of some people then—whereas for Paul, who was, we should remember, an intellectual giant and a Jew, this very fact was part of the glory of the gospel. God was calling all kinds of people from all ranks of society into his kingdom, so that no-one can boast before God (1 Cor. 1:29).

If my intellect could save me (or contribute to my salvation), then I would have something to brag about. If my social status, or the fact that I move among influential people could save me, then I could claim to have a hand in it. But the New Testament proclaims a salvation that is all of God, so that sophisticated and unsophisticated, VIPs and those whom the world counts as nobodies, powerful people and people without any influence— all come to Christ on exactly the same terms: faith in this Lord who at the cross took our sins upon his shoulders and died for us.

The manner of God's working is seen in the composition of his church, and it is the same principle that is seen in the cross itself. Paul says the message of the cross was folly to the Greeks. There is an interesting Greek word that was sometimes applied to the gods—the word *apatheia* (which is behind the English word *apathy*), in its basic meaning of un-suffering, not affected by pain or any other feelings. They thought of their gods as being indifferent to all of that, unable to suffer, and this was one reason why the message of Christ's sufferings on the cross was rejected by them as foolish.

It points up, by way of contrast, the glory of the gospel. The God revealed in Scripture is not apathetic in that sense. He is One who in Christ has come right into this world of suffering and pain, and from the inside he has effected a way of salvation. Far from thinking that God is above all the trials and troubles of this world, the gospel teaches us that the second Person of the Trinity is One who has tasted even death (Heb. 2:9).

Practically and pastorally, there is a huge difference between an attitude that says, 'Take heart, because any gods that exist won't be bothered about little you,' and the reassuring word of a text like 1 Peter 5:7, 'Cast all your anxieties on him, because he cares for you.'

The crucifixion of Jesus, as engineered by Caiaphas and others, is not just about a gigantic miscarriage of justice. It is not simply the cynical victory of expediency over truth. It is God's remedy for sin. He, the innocent One, took our sin upon himself and endured the death that is sin's penalty. The gospel message is well expressed in the old hymn that bids us to rely upon Christ's sacrifice on our behalf:

> When Satan tempts me to despair,
>   And tells me of the guilt within,
> Upward I look and see Him there
>   Who made an end to all my sin.
> Because the sinless Saviour died,
>   My sinful soul is counted free;
> For God the just is satisfied
>   To look on Him and pardon me.[8]

The heart of this gospel, which Caiaphas unwittingly described, is that one Man died so that others could live.

Love so amazing, so divine...

But it is important to remember that this gospel message is not telling us that Jesus, the loving Son, managed to persuade a reluctant Father God to accept us. The whole emphasis of the New Testament is that Christ died for us because God loves us (not that God loves us because Christ died for us).

This is what the New Testament emphasises; it says, 'In Christ God was reconciling the world to himself, not counting their trespasses against them, and entrusting to us the message of reconciliation;' (2 Cor. 5:19) and the apostle John writes, 'The Father has sent his Son to be the Saviour of the world' (1 John 4:14).

[8] Hymn, 'Before the throne of God above' by Charitie Bancroft (1841–92).

We referred earlier to Anselm of Canterbury and his emphasis on the reality and seriousness of sin, and the untainted holiness of God. So (this is how John Stott paraphrased Anselm's answer):

> What can be done? If we are ever to be forgiven, we must repay what we owe. Yet we are incapable of doing this, either for ourselves or for other people. Near the beginning of Book ii, the only possible way out of the human dilemma is unfolded: 'there is no-one… who *can* make this satisfaction except God himself… But no-one *ought* to make it except man; otherwise man does not make the satisfaction'. Therefore, 'it is necessary that one who is God-man should make it. A being who is God and not man, or man and not God, or a mixture of both and therefore neither God nor man, would not qualify. 'It is need-ful that the very same Person who is to make the satisfaction be perfect God and perfect man, since no-one *can* do it except the one who is truly God, and no one *ought* to so it except one who is truly man.[9]

Caiaphas unwittingly referred to the divine answer to the problem: Jesus as this unique God-man has indeed died that others may not die. He bore the punishment we deserve because of our sin, so that he might bring us the forgiveness we do not, and cannot ever, deserve.

So it was that, centuries later, Martin Luther would counsel someone who was distressed by his own sin: 'Learn to know Christ and him crucified. Learn to sing to him and say, "Lord Jesus, you are my righteousness, I am your sin. You took on you what was mine; yet set on me what was yours. You became what you were not, that I might become what I was not."'[10]

Luther's advice to sing it has been taken on board through-out the intervening centuries as hymn after hymn has exulted

---

[9] John Stott, *The Cross of Christ* (Leicester: IVP, 1986), 119.
[10] Quoted in Stott, *Ibid*, 200.

in this message of the cross. The British evangelist, Gypsy Smith (1860–1947), when travelling in New York to preach the gospel, heard someone remark that it was fifty years since Smith had first preached in that city, and he wondered how the man had kept going? Gypsy Smith's answer was, 'I have never lost the wonder of it all.'[11]

This chapter has touched on various aspects of the message of the cross (though much more could be, and has been, said about it[12]), arising from Caiaphas' unintended expression of the gospel.

John tells us that Caiaphas 'did not say this of his own accord' (John 11:51). That doesn't mean that he didn't choose to say what he said. The point is that the deeper meaning of Caiaphas' words didn't come from the speaker's own mind at all. John goes on, 'Being high priest that year he prophesied that Jesus would die for the nation, and not for the nation only, but also to gather into one the children of God who are scattered abroad' (verses 51, 52).

Caiaphas would be astonished to know that his words are remembered all these centuries later. He wanted to put an end to the whole Jesus of Nazareth business; instead, he gives us the gospel according to one of Christ's bitterest enemies. 'It *is* better for you that one man should die for the people, not that the whole nation should perish.' May *we* never lose the wonder of it.

---

[11] Gypsy Smith, quoted in Travis Wiginton, 'Never Lose the Wonder Of It All', *FaithWriters*, 19 December 2007. www.faithwriters.com/article-details.php?id=73530 (accessed 23.8.21).

[12] Anyone writing about the cross of Christ might feel as N. T. Wright felt in writing about the Bible—that it is like building a sandcastle in front of the Matterhorn [quoted in: D. Carson, *Collected Writings on Scripture* (Nottingham: IVP, 2010), 284].

5

Behold Your King!

Some of Jesus' enemies, when they looked at him nailed to the cross, taunted him with the question of why he didn't use his supposedly supernatural power to come down from the cross; if he did that, they said, they would believe in him! They referred to him sarcastically as 'The King of Israel' (Mark 15:32) and this is one of a number of places in the crucifixion narrative where Jesus was described, usually mockingly, as a King:

- Earlier in the same chapter, we are told of the soldiers clothing Jesus in a purple cloak and putting a crown of thorns on his head. Then 'they began to salute him, "Hail, King of the Jews!"' (Mark 15:18). *Some king*, they might have said.

- Luke 23:11 tells of Herod treating Jesus with contempt and arraying him in splendid clothing, and although the *word* 'King' is not found, Herod was mocking the whole idea that Jesus could be any kind of a king.

- The Roman governor, Pontius Pilate, 'wrote an inscription and put it on the cross. It read, "Jesus of Nazareth, the King of the Jews"' (John 19:19).

- Earlier, the same Pilate had paraded the bruised and battered Jesus before the Jews and said, possibly with more contempt for the Jews than for Jesus, 'Behold your King!' (John 19:14).

- The chief priests (who hated the fact that Judea was under Roman rule) answered Pilate, with supreme hypocrisy, 'We have no king but Caesar.'

These references to Jesus as King are further instances of gospel truth being expressed by Jesus' enemies—because the message of the Bible is that he truly is a King, 'the King of kings and Lord of lords' (1 Tim. 6:15).

Perhaps the soldiers would have said they weren't really *enemies* of Jesus; for them, crucifying people was all in a day's work and they possibly thought that Jesus was just another failed revolutionary trying to act against the power of Rome. They simply had the unpleasant task of dispatching him—a horrible job but somebody had to do it! Herod and Pilate also might not have been among Jesus' actual enemies—to them he was perhaps more of a problem to be solved, but they certainly weren't friends of Jesus.

Many a true word is indeed spoken in jest! For the Bible presents him as King indeed; it says that, despite appearances, Jesus' death was the revelation of divine glory: 'being found in human form, he humbled himself by becoming obedient to the point of death, even death on a cross. Therefore God has highly exalted him and bestowed on him the name that is above every name'— the name LORD which, for Jews, was the sacred name of Almighty God and which also signifies 'Master' or 'King'.

Pontius Pilate

John tells us that Pilate and Jesus had spoken about kingship. Pilate asked, 'Are you the King of the Jews?' and Jesus answered,

'My kingdom is not of this world. If my kingdom were of this world, my servants would have been fighting, that I might not be delivered over to the Jews. But my kingdom is not from the world' (John 18:33-36). He spoke about witnessing to the truth and, after Pilate's enigmatic 'What is truth?' (John 18:38), he declared Jesus to be not guilty of any crime.

Later we read about the placard that was attached to his cross. This would normally specify the crime for which a victim was being executed; on this occasion, the notice read, "Jesus of Nazareth, the King of the Jews"' (John 19:19). Pilate had it written in Aramaic, Latin and Greek, the significant languages of that part of the world. Religious art has regularly shown it as 'INRI', representing the Latin form: *Iesus Nazarenus Rex Iudaeorum*.

John seems to have had 'connections', and we read in John 18:15-16 about the priests going to Pilate to object to his wording. They had managed to engineer the death of someone they regarded as a nuisance, a trouble-maker and a threat to the finely balanced peace of the nation (as well as to their position!), and one might have thought they could just let Pilate's jibe pass. But no, they were relentless in their pressuring of Pilate, wanting him to amend the notice to say that Jesus had *claimed to be* the King of the Jews.

Pilate famously answered them, 'What I have written I have written' (John 19:22)—a surprisingly resolute response from someone who had previously prevaricated and shown himself unable (or unwilling) to do the thing that he knew he ought to have done, namely to release Jesus.

He knew that Jesus hadn't done anything to deserve death. In John 18:38-39 he said, 'I find no guilt in him. But you have a custom that I should release one man for you at the Passover. So do you want me to release to you the King of the Jews?' That attempt to extricate himself from his difficulty failed, as did the attempt to have Jesus flogged in the hope that that would satisfy the blood-lust around him (so much for the famous Roman justice).

In John 19:6 we hear Pilate saying again, 'I find no guilt in him' and Luke tells of him sending Jesus off to Herod, tetrarch of Galilee, hoping that Herod could solve his problem by 'taking care' of the Jesus situation (Luke 23:7).

All through, Pilate could not bring himself to do the right thing, partly because there were skeletons rattling in his own cupboard as a result of misjudgements he had made in his administration of Judea.

He must have been an able man to be appointed a governor in the first place, and then to be sent to Judea in particular, since that was a troublesome part of the empire. But one thing that he did not have was respect for the people he had been sent to govern.

His first action on arriving in Judea was to set up Roman standards in Jerusalem with the image of Caesar on them, something which previous governors had avoided out of deference to the Jews, with their well-known commandment against idolatry. When the Jews resisted and Pilate threatened to kill them all, they called his bluff and he eventually had to climb down and remove the images. Later he took money from the temple to fund the construction of an aqueduct. This provoked further demonstrations, which led Pilate to give the order for troops to be sent among the crowd, and then at a given signal they massacred many by the sword.

These are examples of the maladministration which left him in a position where he had to tread warily, lest further bad reports should go to Rome (a guy has to safeguard his career, after all).[1]

---

[1] Later complaints against Pilate resulted in his being summoned to explain himself before the emperor. Nothing is known of the outcome of the hearing; one report says that Pilate was eventually forced into committing suicide.

And after he had eventually been manoeuvred into complying with the desires of Jesus' powerful enemies, he came out with this piece of uncharacteristic resolution: 'What I have written I have written.' He had staged the ridiculous charade of literally washing his hands before the crowd and saying, 'I am innocent of this man's blood' (Matt. 27:24), but through the centuries people have known his name from the regular recitation of the phrase of the Apostles' Creed: '...suffered under Pontius Pilate, was crucified, dead and buried.'

Dramatic irony can hardly go further—here in 'Jesus of Nazareth, the King of the Jews' is the ultimate truth, conveyed by none other than Pontius Pilate, the representative of worldly power in Judea. It is, as we say, rich, after all that has gone before; it is also wonderful that this apparent triumph of wickedness and evil, when it looked as if the devil and hell had won the day, was in fact the crux of God's saving plan.

The writing on the cross

When someone was sentenced to be crucified, a soldier would walk in front of the condemned with a placard stating the crime for which they were being executed. They would pass through as many streets as possible to ensure that the masses would see what happened to people who offended Rome. It also provided a last chance for anyone who could still produce evidence that might prove the convict's innocence to speak up, in which case the procession would be stopped and the case re-opened. When they got to the place of execution, the notice would be nailed to the cross.

John's gospel tells us, 'Many of the Jews read this inscription, for the place where Jesus was crucified was near the city, and it was written in Aramaic, in Latin, and in Greek' (John 19:20).

Perhaps John drew attention to this detail because it seemed to him to be a sign of Jesus' universal kingship. The placard seemed to say: whatever language you use, this truly is the king. Whether it's in Aramaic, Latin or Greek—or in Arabic, Lithuanian or Gaelic—this is the message of the gospel, nailed down by order of the Roman governor.

Later, Paul drew out this *gospel according to Christ's enemies* when he wrote about forgiveness through the cross as the cancellation of 'the record of debt that stood against us' which Jesus 'set aside, nailing it to the cross. He disarmed the rulers and authorities and put them to open shame, by triumphing over them in him' (Col. 2:13-15).

He would have learned what the actual wording was, but he was saying: in another sense it was our sin that was written up there on the cross. The Greek word translated as 'record of debt' literally means hand-writing, and Paul's bold metaphor says that when the anonymous Roman soldier nailed the board to the cross, God was setting aside our debt, 'nailing it to the cross.'

This was not simply one of the world's most terrible miscarriages of justice; it was not merely the removal of one more in the series of rebels against Rome in those rough and tough days; it was not only an instance of suffering and death nobly borne in martyrdom. This was the triune God himself nailing our sins to the cross—greater love has no-one than this (John 15:13).

And when he said, 'It is finished' (one word in Greek—John 19:30), he meant that he had completed the task of taking our sin upon himself and driving a nail through our 'IOU'.

Paul used many images to convey the truth of the gospel, and another which he used in Colossians is the image of a Roman Triumph. He wrote about God disarming the rulers and authorities and putting them to open shame (The New International Version puts it 'made a public spectacle of them'), by triumphing over them in Christ (Col. 2:15).

Crucifixion was intended, among other things, to humiliate the victim and to warn subjugated people about what would happen to you if you took up arms against Rome. But Paul alluded to the procession of a general returning home after a successful campaign, parading his victorious army for the crowds to see and cheer. In the procession there would be soldiers, musicians—and prisoners, evidence of his victory. And Paul says that in the crucifixion which was supposed to make a public spectacle of Jesus, Jesus was actually making a public spectacle of the forces of sin and wickedness. It was a remarkable claim, because on that dark Friday it looked as if his enemies had triumphed over Jesus. They had attacked him, criticised him, hounded him, and now they had prevailed over him.

But Paul combined these vivid pictures to draw out what was happening at Calvary: God himself nailing our sins to the cross, cancelling our IOU and triumphing over sin, death and hell.

Poor Pontius Pilate had no idea what he was saying when he brought out the beaten and bruised Jesus to the crowds and said, 'Behold your King!' (John 19:14) or when he ordered that sign to read: 'Jesus of Nazareth, the King of the Jews.'

Jesus is Lord

Jesus truly is the King. The theme is stated right at the beginning of the New Testament as Matthew tells of the quest of the wise men: 'Where is he who has been born king of the Jews?' (Matt. 2:2), a saying which greatly troubled the Jewish King Herod who was nervous about any potential rival.

Soon after the events of Jesus' death and resurrection, his followers faced challenges in relation to their allegiance to Jesus as Lord. The phrase 'Jesus is Lord' was one of the earliest Christian assertions, and it means '*Jesus* is Lord—not anyone or anything else.' The first loyalty of a Christian is to the Lord Christ. Jesus himself said that his followers should 'render to Caesar the things that are Caesar's'—which is a mandate for good citizenship—but he went on to say, perhaps with emphasis, '*and* to God the things that are God's' (Luke 20:25).

The New Testament shows this principle being worked out in both word and action. As to the first, Peter wrote, 'Be subject for the Lord's sake to every human institution, whether it be to the emperor as supreme, or to governors as sent by him' (1 Pet. 2:13-14), and as for the second, we see it in action in Acts 5 when Peter and John were ordered to refrain from speaking about Jesus; their reply was, 'We must obey God rather than men' (Acts 5:29).

So discipleship leads to good citizenship, but that citizenship is subject to our higher allegiance to Christ. I once visited a church in Jerusalem and picked up a magazine with an article written by the pastor. He referred to Paul's use of the phrase (using the Hebrew name for Jesus) 'Yeshua is Lord' (Rom. 10:9):

> His use of the phrase was most likely chosen by Paul to make it certain to the would-be believer that Caesar is no longer. Unlike so many who use this verse to make it 'easy' to enter the kingdom, the Roman man would have understood that Paul was demanding that he risk his very life to enter the kingdom. Whenever a Roman citizen declared 'Caesar is Lord', he was confessing his ultimate loyalty to Rome. He was not merely saying words; he was saying that there is none greater than Rome, and his life was committed to serving the

Roman world. If someone refused to honour Caesar as God and confess him as Lord he was risking his very life.[2]

It is a pressure that has come at many times and in many ways to faithful believers. During the period before the Second World War, there were many professing Christians in Germany who followed a policy of fitting in with Nazism, but on the other hand there was the 'Confessing Church'. One of its pastors was Martin Niemöller.

On one occasion some members of the *Hitlerjugend* (Hitler Youth) threw a bomb into the parsonage after the pastor had preached a sermon with the title (emphasis on the first word), '*Gott ist mein Führer.*' It doesn't take much linguistic ability to translate that into English, and it was a statement that was highly significant because of Hitler's use of that very title *Führer* (leader). Niemöller's message, when he said "*Gott ist mein Führer*" was— God, not Hitler, is my Leader, my Master, my Lord. Obviously that was dynamite, and it led to his arrest and imprisonment in Sachsenhausen and Dachau from 1937–45.

Websites such as those of Barnabas Fund, Christian Solidarity Worldwide and Steadfast Global give much information about the persecution of Christians in many parts of today's world. And in the supposedly tolerant and democratic western world also, it is a radical step to be openly known as a committed Christian. It is counter-cultural, which means going against the trend in contemporary society. It means saying my lord and master is not money, it is not pleasure and it is not the state—*Jesus* is my Master.

Lord of all

Jesus' call is a demanding one. It is not merely a matter of taking on a religious aspect of life or honouring him in one compartment

---

[2] Pastoral letter of Wayne Hilsden in the April 2008 issue of the magazine of King of Kings Church, Jerusalem.

of our activities. Christianity is about complete surrender to the authority of Christ as our Lord and Master.

The New Testament would reject altogether any notion of receiving Jesus as Saviour but not as Lord, or receiving him as Saviour now and as Lord at some future time, as if (in Samuel Rutherford's phrase) we would 'have Christ divided into two halves, that we might take the half of him only! We take Jesus and salvation; but "Lord" is a cumbersome word…'[3] Jesus Christ is Lord of all, or he is not Lord at all.

When Jesus was mockingly called king by the religious and political authorities; by the soldiers doing their day's shift, by Herod in all his contempt and by the vacillating Pontius Pilate, the truth of the gospel was indeed expressed by Jesus' enemies. They said much more than they knew, for, long after they have disappeared from the scene, Jesus remains 'King for ever' (Psa. 10:16; 29:10).

Pilate probably would have thought that the kingdom he served would stand and grow for ever; what hope was there for this poor battered man with no possessions, no power and so pitifully few followers (and few of them people who 'mattered')? Yet it's true; Rome collapsed and Pilate's name would never have been remembered if he hadn't met Jesus. Throughout the centuries, many efforts have been made to eradicate Christianity and do away with the very name of Jesus, yet it is his kingdom that stands and grows.

An enduring kingdom

Among the so-called 'new atheists' of the early twenty-first century, one writer, Richard Dawkins, expressed the hope that after

---

[3] *Letters of Samuel Rutherford* (Edinburgh: Banner of Truth, 1973), 132.

people had read his book, entitled *The God Delusion*, they would be convinced atheists. In an interesting twist, the comedian Marcus Brigstocke commented, 'I was an atheist when I started reading *The God Delusion*; by the time I had finished it I was an agnostic. I was going to read it again but I worried that I might turn into a fundamentalist Christian.'[4]

The Psalms suggest that God smiles at the futile arrogance of little human beings who 'take him on.' Psalm 2, for example, says, 'Why do the nations rage and the peoples plot in vain? The kings of the earth set themselves, and the rulers take counsel together against the LORD and his Anointed,' but 'He who sits in the heavens laughs.'

Of course such verses have to be set alongside many others which speak of the Lord as compassionate and long-suffering (for example, Psa. 103:8-14) and not wishing that any should perish (for example, 2 Pet. 3:9). In Ezekiel 37:11 we have God's word: 'I have no pleasure in the death of the wicked, but that the wicked turn from his way and live.' Even on the verge of his own maltreatment in Jerusalem, we read about Jesus that 'when he drew near and saw the city, he wept over it, saying, "Would that you, even you, had known on this day the things that make for peace!"' (Luke 19:41, 42).

It is in trusting and obeying him that the way of blessedness is found. A famous hymn makes the point that captivity to Christ is true freedom. This is the paradox that is missed by so many who think that freedom from the restraints of obedience brings happiness and liberation. Jesus said, 'Everyone who practises sin is a slave to sin…[but] if the Son sets you free, you will be free indeed' (John 8:34-36). The paradox of the matter is:

[4] M. Brigstocke, *God Collar* (London: Bantam Books, 2011), 156.

> My will is not my own
>   Till Thou hast made it Thine;
> If it would reach a monarch's throne
>   It must its crown resign.[5]

A violin string lying on a table is free and subject to no force. But it is not free to make beautiful music; it is just a piece of metal, nylon or gut. However, if you take it and insert it into a violin and stretch it, then it is firmly bound but it is then free to do what a violin string is meant for: to make fine music. Submission to the kingship of Christ brings freedom to live the lives we are meant to live.

In the world there are different kinds of kingship, and the novelist Philip Pullman, in responding to a question about his rejection of what he called an 'authoritative religion', said that he prefers to speak of the republic of heaven! 'I don't want to do without heaven, but I can no longer believe in a Kingdom of heaven. So there must be a republic of heaven of which we are free and equal citizens.'[6]

Well, whatever one's views may be in the political and social realm, republicanism does not exist in Christ's realm. He is an absolute monarch—but of course he is also love. Romans 1:5 speaks about 'the obedience of faith' and 1 John 5:3 spells out the effect of such obedience: 'This is the love of God, that we keep his commandments. And his commandments are not burdensome.'

When Pontius Pilate brought Jesus out to the crowds and said, 'Behold your King!' (John 19:14), he was mocking the people who suggested that Jesus was a danger to Roman power, but he gave expression to *the gospel according to Christ's enemies.*

[5] Hymn, 'Make me a captive, Lord' by George Matheson (1842–1906).
[6] Joan Bakewell (ed.), *Belief* (London: Duckworth, 2005), 179.

And we close this chapter with a meditative poem on the theme of Christ's Kingship:

> A king? They call Him King! Is homage due
> To such a one? A king? Can it be true?
> The lowly Jew, born in far Bethlehem?
> Men from all nations say He died for them
> And rose from Death, to hold a heavenly sway
> To which all men must bow the knee some day.
>
> The king? If King of Heaven, had He no power
> To stay the surging evil of that hour?
> He had—but out He went, and there He died
> That sinners might be cleansed and justified,
> Brought back to God. The wonder of this thing–
> A pauper's pardon purchased by a King
> The King. Today this question comes anew–
> Will you have Jesus to reign over you?
> His hands and feet are pierced, his brow is scarred
> But there is Glory in that face once marred.
> He reigns! His claims come ringing, challenging–
> Will you have Jesus Christ to be your King?[7]

P. S.

As a post-script to this chapter we might also refer to the last biblical appearance of Pilate, as told at the end of Matthew 27. The chief priests and Pharisees came to Pilate and referred to 'that impostor' who had said, 'After three days I will rise.' They wanted to avoid the possibility of Jesus' disciples coming to steal the body and then concocting a story about him rising from the dead.

Pilate's response was to grant them a detachment of soldiers. And then he said, 'Go, make it as secure as you can.' Is it one last

[7] Maurice Cox in *Jesus Is Alive: Gospel Themes and Scripts by the Kairos Group* (London: Falcon Books, 1972), 123f.

jibe from Pilate? These enemies of Christ were still not satisfied and it's as if Pilate says to them: *Keep Christ in the tomb—if you can!*

6

That's Not What We Meant!

Another striking example of dramatic irony is found in Mark's account of the crucifixion. He tells of passers-by deriding Jesus and challenging him to save himself. The chief priests and the scribes joined in the mockery and said, 'He saved others; he cannot save himself' (Mark 15:29-31).

In this chapter we consider these two ironic phrases, 'He saved others' and 'He cannot save himself.'

'He saved others'

Never was a truer word spoken.

Perhaps they pointed to the board above the cross that was meant to announce the crime for which he was being executed—'The King of the Jews' (Mark 15:26)—and out came their snide contempt: *let this King of Israel save himself.*

But when they said 'He saved others', they never said a truer word. Saving people was the reason for his coming; it had been the reality of his ministry and it would continue as the relevance of his gospel.

First it was *the reason for his coming.*

He said, referring to himself by his preferred title, 'The Son of Man came to seek and to save the lost' (Luke 19:10). He said, 'God did not send his Son into the world to condemn the world, but in order that the world might be saved through him' (John 3:17). He said, 'I did not come to judge the world but to save the world' (John 12:47).

The whole message of the Bible centres in God's work for the salvation of a world gone wrong. He did not come, as some have supposed, simply to give an example of the good and moral life, or of how to be patient while suffering injustice. He did not come to leave a legacy of admirable teaching, or to establish a new society dedicated to helping people live better lives.

Such ideas may contain elements of truth, but the main thing is that the gospel is a message of salvation—salvation that affects all three tenses: it is a past fact, a present reality and a future hope.

It is a past fact in the sense that it depends on the incarnation of Christ and the atonement brought about by his death in the place of sinners. This is what the apostle Paul stated so plainly; after all his attempts to wipe out Christianity and after his whole life was turned around on the road to Damascus, he would write, 'Christ Jesus came into the world to save sinners' (1 Tim. 1:15). The very word 'Jesus' *means* Saviour (Matt. 1:21) and the word 'Christ' is not so much a name as a title, corresponding to the Hebrew word *Messiah* and referring to the 'Anointed One'.

In Old Testament times, three groups of people were anointed for their office: prophets, priests and kings, and Jesus is presented by the Bible as the Prophet who teaches us what we need to know, as the High Priest who presents himself to the Father as an atoning sacrifice, and as the King whom we are called to obey. This 'Christ Jesus', the apostle says, came into the world to save—to save sinners, and Paul goes on, '...of whom I am the foremost.

But I received mercy for this reason, that in me, as the foremost, Jesus Christ might display his perfect patience as an example to those who were to believe in him for eternal life' (1 Tim. 1:15, 16). Salvation centres in this event of the cross through which indeed he 'saved others' in a way that his mocking enemies didn't realise.

Salvation is also a present reality, and Christians can be described as those who *are being saved*. That's how the early church is described by Luke: 'The Lord added to their number day by day those who were being saved' (Acts 2:47). The salvation which becomes real when a sinner turns to Christ in repentance and faith is also the beginning of a saved life, in which we are to 'work out' that salvation (Phil. 2:12).

And it is also, of course, a future hope, in that salvation will be completed when we are brought into his nearer presence after this life is over when the ransomed of the Lord will enjoy the fulness of salvation in his presence where there are joys for evermore (Psa. 16:11). Many people dismiss this aspect of biblical teaching as a pious dream, but it is a sure part of the salvation of Christ. This is a hope that burns within the hearts of Christians.

Saving others was the reason for Christ's coming. It was also *the reality of his ministry.*

When his enemies said, 'He saved others', they were mocking the whole concept—probably not only the concept of people being saved but the idea that *he*, a penniless carpenter's son from backwater Nazareth, might be able to save anyone!

However, they spoke the truth. It had been happening throughout the three-year period of his public ministry. For example, in Luke 7:50 we hear him saying to a woman who had previously been living a sinful life, 'Your faith has saved you; go in peace.' This is the kind of occurrence and the kind of person that the priests were meaning when they mocked Jesus on the cross saying, 'He saved others.' He certainly did! That woman would testify to it, as would those who had known her previous way of life and who would see the radical change brought about by the salvation of Christ.

Another notable instance was little Zacchaeus, to whom we have referred previously. He too was known as someone who had been 'saved' by Jesus, as his enemies disparagingly put it. Zacchaeus was a tax collector working for the occupying power and, as such, would be *persona non grata* among most Jews, religious or not. But he was curious to see Jesus, and then shocked as Jesus called out to him in his arboreal hiding place, saying that he would visit Zacchaeus' house.

It was an encounter that changed his life, and we hear him saying, 'Half of my goods I give to the poor. And if I have defrauded anyone of anything' (many would have interjected, 'What do you mean "if"!'), I restore it fourfold.' This was the sign of his changed life, his new priorities, his saved life. It's what Jesus said: 'Today salvation has come to this house…For the Son of Man came to seek and to save the lost' (Luke 19: 1, 10).

And there were many others: the disciple Matthew, blind Bartimaeus, the paralyzed man of Mark 2, the leper of Luke 17, the Samaritan woman, and (from the other end of the social and religious spectrum) Nicodemus, to whom Jesus spoke about his purpose that 'whoever believes in him should not perish but have eternal life. For God did not send his Son into the world to condemn the world, but in order that the world might be saved through him' (John 3:16, 17).

Saving others was the reason for his coming; it had been the reality of his ministry; and it would continue as *the relevance of his gospel.*

The Bible is not merely about historical events which can be viewed with the detached interest of an antiquarian. At the very beginning of Acts, Luke referred to the gospel he had written and said that he had 'dealt with all that Jesus began to do and teach until the day when he was taken up', with the clear implication that he planned to tell in Acts of the things that Jesus *continued* to do, whether referring to large numbers such as the three thousand people who were converted on the day of Pentecost (Acts 2:41), or an individual like the lame beggar in the chapter after that. More and more people were added to the church, like the three remarkably different characters in Acts 16: the well-to-do businesswoman Lydia, the demented slave-girl and the Philippian jailor.

In derision they mocked him, saying, 'He saved others'—but it was wonderfully true—and it still is. This message of salvation has been proclaimed through the centuries and lives have been saved and changed through the same gospel of Christ.

Examples could be adduced by the thousand; people such as the former slave-trader John Newton who wrote about the amazing grace which saved a wretch like himself and who wrote his own epitaph, describing himself as 'once an infidel and libertine, a servant of slaves in Africa, (who) was by the rich mercy of our Lord and Saviour Jesus Christ, preserved, restored, pardoned, and appointed to preach the faith he had long laboured to destroy.'

In more recent times, take the case of the former British Cabinet minister, Jonathan Aitken, who was convicted and imprisoned for perjury, but then saved by the grace of Christ. In his autobiography he wrote about treading on holy ground—

> …I am still too full of awe and wonder to be able to write clearly about what has happened. I am not even capable of saying when it happened, for I cannot point to a blinding flash of light on the road to Damascus, nor to an instant moment of

conversion. Yet somewhere along the painful road of the journey described in this book, after many months of prayer and listening, my eyes opened and I recognised that I had accepted Jesus Christ into my heart as my Lord and my God.[1]

When Jesus' enemies said, 'He saved others', they meant it as an insult but they spoke the truth. He had indeed been saving people, and he is still doing so.

Some people baulk at the language of salvation and being saved, but there should be no embarrassment about it, because it was the reason for Jesus' coming into the world—to save sinners.

Similarly some people feel awkward about the language of being converted or born again. I remember hearing of a lady who was rather exasperated by such talk, and once in a small group meeting she burst out with, 'What's all this about being "born again"? What on earth does it mean?' Someone explained that it was all about turning from one's sin and self-centredness and praying that the risen Lord would come into one's life and bring forgiveness, peace and the promise of eternal life. The lady thought for a moment and then said, 'Oh… Oh…Well, in that case I'm born again'! She simply hadn't realised the meaning of the words but she *had* turned to Christ in repentance and faith.

That's how this great message of salvation becomes ours. As Paul explained, 'If you confess with your mouth that Jesus is Lord and believe in your heart that God raised him from the dead, you will be saved' (Rom. 10:9).

'He cannot save himself'

When his enemies said that he couldn't save himself, they clearly meant that, once Jesus had been nailed to the cross, there

[1] *Pride and Perjury* (London: Harper Collins, 2000), 361.

was nothing he could do. They had engineered his betrayal, arrest, mock trials and now crucifixion. They had seen and heard horrible nails being driven through his hands and feet and then he was left there, helpless and defenceless—as a Christian poet has expressed it, 'stranded, halfway between hilltop and heaven (neither will have you).'[2]

That phrase 'neither will have you' takes us to the heart of the gospel. He was not only 'despised and rejected by men' (Isa. 53:3); he was also the One who cried out, 'My God, why have you forsaken me?' (Mark 15:34). The irony of his enemies' words about his inability to save himself lies in the Bible's teaching that if he was to accomplish the divine plan he must drink the cup of suffering to the dregs. That's what he prayed in the garden of Gethsemane: 'Abba, Father, all things are possible for you. Remove this cup from me'—and then he added, 'Yet not what I will, but what you will' (Mark 14:36).

The whole emphasis of the Bible is that, humanly speaking, he *could* have avoided it all. Luke 9:51 tells of a time when 'he set his face to go to Jerusalem' and that is prefaced by, 'When the days drew near for him to be taken up…', which presumably refers to the ascension of the risen Christ. Luke was indicating that Jesus not only knew what lay ahead, but that he was really in control of events.

On another occasion, the disciples tried to warn Jesus of the dangers that would face him if he went to the capital. It was the time when he heard of Lazarus' illness and he said, 'Let us go to Judea again.' His disciples remonstrated with him: 'Rabbi, the Jews there were just now seeking to stone you, and are you going there again?' The pessimistic Thomas even resigned himself to

---

[2] Luci Shaw, *The Revolutionary*, quoted in *Christian Graduate*, December 1980.

what might lie ahead, saying with resolution, 'Let us also go' and then he added, 'that we may die with him.' He could see no good coming of it, but he would still be loyal. And all through there is the figure of Jesus who had his eyes wide open.

And there were occasions when he spoke plainly about it. The occasion at Caesarea Philippi when Jesus questioned the disciples about their understanding of his person is regarded as a watershed moment in Mark's gospel. After Peter's confession of faith in him as the Christ (or Messiah), Mark tells us, 'He began to teach them that the Son of Man must suffer many things and be rejected by the elders and the chief priests and the scribes and be killed, and after three days rise again. And he said this plainly' (Mark 8:31-32).

Again, in Mark 9:31, 'He was teaching his disciples, saying to them, "The Son of Man is going to be delivered into the hands of men, and they will kill him. And when he is killed, after three days he will rise."' Mark adds, 'But they did not understand the saying, and were afraid to ask him.' It is not surprising that they couldn't get the hang of what he was telling them: why would he run any risk of going to a place where he could be apprehended and so treated, and as for the idea of resurrection, that was obviously nonsensical!

There was a third time when Jesus spoke about his coming death:

> And they were on the road, going up to Jerusalem, and Jesus was walking ahead of them. And they were amazed, and those who followed were afraid. And taking the twelve again, he began to tell them what was going to happen to him, saying, 'See, we are going up to Jerusalem, and the Son of Man will be delivered over to the chief priests and the scribes, and they will condemn him to death and deliver him over to the Gentiles.

And they will mock him and spit on him, and flog him and kill him. And after three days he will rise' (Mark 10:32-34).

He had certainly forewarned them; nothing that happened took Jesus by surprise. But the disciples couldn't take it in.

Humanly speaking, he could have saved himself from it all. How? He could have stayed away from Jerusalem; he could have avoided controversy with the Jewish religious leaders; he could have called down heavenly assistance, for even at the time of his arrest, when Peter intervened with a sword, he said, 'Do you think that I cannot appeal to my Father, and he will at once send me more than twelve legions of angels?[3] But how then should the Scriptures be fulfilled, that it must be so?' (Matthew 27:53, 54).

In C. S. Lewis's famous story of Aslan, there is the point at which the great lion has been captured, and:

> Lucy and Susan held their breaths waiting for Aslan's roar and his spring upon his enemies. But it never came. Four Hags, grinning and leering, yet also (at first) hanging back and half afraid of what they had to do, had approached him. 'Bind him, I say!' repeated the White Witch. The Hags made a dart at him and shrieked with triumph when they found that he made no resistance at all. Then others—evil dwarfs and apes—rushed in to help them, and between them they rolled the huge Lion over on his back and tied all his four paws together, shouting and cheering as if they had done something brave, though, had the Lion chosen, one of these paws could have been the death of them all.[4]

The last phrase of Matthew 27:54 brings us to the crux of the matter—'it must be so.' When Jesus said, 'The Son of Man must

---

[3] That is, more than 72,000 of them!

[4] C. S. Lewis, *The Lion, the Witch and the Wardrobe* (Harmondsworth: Penguin Books, 1978), 138.

suffer many things and be killed', the word 'must' does not refer to the betrayal of Judas, the malice of the Jewish authorities, the weakness of Pilate or the cruelty of soldiers. The 'must' refers to a divine, not earthly, necessity. Throughout all the events leading up to his crucifixion, Jesus did not offer any kind of physical resistance—all because 'it must be so'; it was the culmination of a divine plan.

This theme is expressed in the words of a hymn that asks whether it was the nails that bound him to the tree and answers that it was rather his everlasting love.[5] 1 John 4:10 expresses this when it says, 'He loved us and sent his Son to be the propitiation for our sins.'

This emphasis has been expounded by the late John Stott in his epic book on the cross where he wrote that, although Jesus knew he must die, '…it was not because he was the helpless victim of evil forces arrayed against him, or of any inflexible fate decreed for him, but because he freely embraced the purpose of his Father for the salvation of sinners, as it had been revealed in Scripture.'[6]

In John 12:27 we are allowed to overhear Jesus praying to his Father. He said, 'Now is my soul troubled. And what shall I say? "Father, save me from this hour"? But for this purpose I have come to this hour. Father glorify your name.' This ties in with what he had already been teaching them.

The whole purpose of his coming, his incarnation, was that he might offer a once-for-all sacrifice for sin. The Bible tells us, 'The wages of sin is death' (Rom. 6:23), and Jesus' work was to accept these wages, to bear that penalty, in his own body on the tree (1 Pet. 2:24). The hymn-writer expresses it in song:

[5] Hymn *Give me a sight, O Saviour* by Katherine A. M. Kelly (1869–1942).
[6] J. Stott, *The Cross of Christ* (Leicester: IVP, 1986), 32.

Man of Sorrows! Wondrous name
   For the Son of God, who came
Ruined sinners to reclaim!
   Hallelujah! What a Saviour!

Bearing shame and scoffing rude,
   In my place condemned He stood,
Sealed my pardon with His blood:
   Hallelujah! What a Saviour![7]

When his enemies said, 'He cannot save himself,' they were unwittingly expressing the deepest truth. They might even have referred to their Old Testament and the text we quoted earlier that says, 'Cursed be everyone who is hanged on a tree' (Deut. 21:23). They hadn't realised that this could actually be God's way, that that very verse about a crucified person being cursed might be answered by Galatians 3:13 where Paul wrote, 'Christ redeemed us from the curse of the law by becoming a curse for us, for it is written, "Cursed is everyone who is hung on a tree."'

And after his mission was 'finished' (John 19:30), he rose from the dead and appeared to many of them, including the two disciples on the road to Emmaus. Explaining what had happened, he said, 'Was it not necessary that the Christ should suffer these things and enter into his glory?' And then, 'Beginning with Moses and all the Prophets, he interpreted to them in all the Scriptures the things concerning himself' (Luke 24:26, 27).

One commentator has written:

> The word *all* is probably important. They had no doubt seized on the prediction of the glory of the Messiah, but it was quite another thing to take to heart the prophecies that pointed to the darker side of his mission. But the dark side was there, in the prophecies. And this means that the passion

---

[7] Hymn, 'Man of Sorrows!' by Philip Bliss (1838–76).

was not simply a possibility that might or might not become actual, depending on the circumstances: it was *necessary...* Luke gives no indication of which passages the Lord chose, but he makes it clear that the whole Old Testament was involved. We should perhaps understand this not as the selection of a number of proof-texts, but rather as showing that throughout the Old Testament a consistent divine purpose is worked out, a purpose that in the end meant and must mean the cross. The terribleness of sin is found throughout the Old Testament and so is the deep, deep love of God. In the end this combination made Calvary inevitable.[8]

His enemies said, 'He saved others; he cannot save himself' (Mark 15:29-31) and if they had read any of what has been written above, they would have protested, 'But that's not what we meant!'

But he *did* save others and he *didn't* save himself. They said, 'Let the Christ, the King of Israel, come down now from the cross that we may see and believe' (Mark 15:32)—but, as is often said, it is because he did not come down from the cross that we believe in him.

He went all the way to death for us. As the perfect God-Man, he came to save people indeed: because he was divine he could *save* us; because he was human he could save *us*.

---

[8] Leon Morris, *Tyndale New Testament Commentary on Luke* (Leicester: IVP, 1974), 338-9.

7

To Save Sinners

So far we have been considering the gospel according to people who were out-and-out enemies of Christ. This chapter, however, is about the gospel according to a man who *used to be* an enemy of Christ, but his life was changed and instead of being a persecutor of Christ and Christianity, he became a missionary and minister of Christ. It's about Saul of Tarsus who became the apostle Paul.

Although he possibly did more (from the human point of view) for the spread of Christianity than anyone else in that ancient world, and although it became his great ambition to preach the gospel where the name of Christ was unknown (Rom. 15:20), Paul started off as one of the fiercest enemies of Christ. Before his whole world was turned upside down on the road to Damascus (Acts 9), his life had been devoted to the elimination of Christianity.

Paul the persecutor

The first time we hear of Paul (or Saul as he was then) is in connection with the earliest Christian martyrdom. Stephen, 'a man full of faith and of the Holy Spirit' (Acts 6:5), had been seized and brought before the Jewish council, charged with speaking against the temple and the Jewish law, and saying that Jesus of Nazareth would 'destroy this place and change the customs that Moses delivered to us' (Acts 6:14).

Chapter 7 of Acts gives the record of his speech before the Jewish Council, in which he emphasised the point that God had revealed himself and spoken to people in many places *outwith the temple*, for 'the Most High does not dwell in houses made by hands' (Acts 7:48).

Then, without bothering about the niceties of proper procedure and the passing of disinterested verdicts, they 'cast him out of the city and stoned him,' (Acts 7:58) and this is where Paul makes his first appearance. We are told that he held the garments of those who stoned Stephen as he died praying for the forgiveness of his enemies.

The next chapter begins, 'And Saul approved of his execution' (Acts 8:1).

Luke then goes on to tell of how he ravaged the church 'and entering house after house, he dragged off men and women and committed them to prison.' Later, when speaking before the Jewish king Agrippa, he referred back to the way in which he had sought to do his duty as he saw it at that time:

> I myself was convinced that I ought to do many things in opposing the name of Jesus of Nazareth. And I did so in Jerusalem. I not only locked up many of the saints in prison after receiving authority from the chief priests, but when they were put to death I cast my vote against them. And I punished them often in all the synagogues and tried to make them blaspheme, and in raging fury against them I persecuted them even to foreign cities (Acts 26:9-11).

There is no doubt that Saul started off as one of the fiercest enemies of Christianity.

Paul the convert

Everything changed for Paul on the day that is described by Luke in Acts 9, and later by Paul himself in chapters 22 and 26 of Acts. After telling of Saul's approval of Stephen's martyrdom, Luke breaks off to tell of events in Samaria, before coming back to Saul in 9:1—'still breathing threats and murder against the disciples of the Lord.'

For anyone reading the words for the first time, the change that followed could hardly be more dramatic and unexpected. He might have told his story:

I was going along the road, with my letters of authorisation from the High Priest—because I had heard that there were some Christians (misguided fools) in Damascus and I thought 'We'll soon deal with them.' I sincerely believed that Christianity was a dangerous heresy and that God wanted me to crush it. And then in a moment my whole life changed. There was this light that shone on me and I found myself on the ground, unable to see anything but I heard a voice—and I just knew whose voice it was—saying to me, 'Saul, Saul, why are you persecuting Me?' My whole life was changed in that moment.

Paul came *from* a position of violent opposition to the very name of Jesus *to* a position of believing in him and accepting him as Saviour and Lord. As he would express it later, 'I was a blasphemer, persecutor and insolent opponent. But I received mercy because I had acted ignorantly in unbelief, and the grace of our Lord overflowed for me with the faith and love that are in Christ Jesus' (1 Tim. 1:12-14).

C. S. Lewis famously described himself as 'the most reluctant convert in all England'[1]; something similar might once have been

---

[1] C. S. Lewis, *Surprised by Joy* (London: Geoffrey Bles, 1955), 182.

written by Paul—he might have called himself the most reluctant convert in all Judea, and if we had seen anything of Paul in these days when he was seeking to wipe Christianity off the face of the earth, we probably would have said, 'There's one person who'll never be a Christian.'

And from his own experience, Paul might say to us: *Don't write anybody off. There will be people of whom you might be inclined to say, 'Well, that's someone who'll never become a Christian.' Never say never. Doesn't my story tell you that you should never draw such a conclusion; you won't win everyone, but don't write anybody off.*

The circumstances and surroundings may be very different, and when Paul described his own conversion as an 'example to those who were to believe in him for eternal life' (1 Tim. 1:16; the King James Version uses the word 'pattern'), he clearly did not mean that every conversion would involve being struck to the ground and rendered temporarily blind. The outward circumstances will probably be different, but Paul's own experience convinced him that God can break into people's lives and change them altogether. 'If anyone is in Christ', he would write, 'he is a new creation' (2 Cor. 5:17).

For Paul it was the beginning of a new life; it led to a new way of thinking; it gave him a new mission; and it involved a new challenge.

A new life

What happened that day marked the end of Paul's days as an enemy of Christ; it marked the beginning of a new life. The Bible frequently uses the word 'repent', which means *about-turn*—you were going in one direction and you turn round and go in the opposite direction. In his speech before King Agrippa, Paul described his own ministry as one which called people to 'repent and turn to God, performing deeds in keeping with their repentance' (Acts 26:20).

Earlier, John the Baptist had said a similar thing: 'Bear fruits in keeping with repentance' (Luke 3:8). When he was asked what that meant, he gave some very specific, down-to-earth examples of what it would mean: sharing your wealth with others, acting with complete integrity and honesty, and living a life of contentment. The New Testament as a whole draws out many ways in which repentance will manifest itself in a person's life. Any idea of Christian conversion as a momentary or fleeting experience that gives assurance of eternal life but makes no difference to life in this world is a sham and is counterfeit.

Paul characterised conversion as the *beginning* of God's good work in the life of the believer (Phil. 1:6). No one is made perfect by some kind of spiritual jet propulsion, and when the famous John Bunyan wrote the book which has become the world's second bestseller (next to the Bible[2]), he characterised the Christian life as a *Pilgrim's Progress,* with many struggles along the way. Paul wrote of the constant battle against his fallen human nature.

Paul rejoiced in the fact that there is 'now no condemnation for those who are in Christ Jesus' (Rom. 8:1), but he also recognised God's calling to grow in Christ-likeness. God sent his Son to condemn sin in the flesh; as he wrote, 'in order that the righteous requirements of the law might be fulfilled in us, who walk not according to the flesh but according to the Spirit' (Rom. 8:3-4).

A Puritan writer called Samuel Bolton, commenting on that teaching, said that the law (all that the Bible says about the way we ought to live) sends us to the gospel that we may be justified

---

[2] *The Pilgrim's Progress* was published in 1678; it has been translated into 200 languages and it has never been out of print.

(because we cannot make ourselves good enough), and then the gospel sends us to the law of God that we may know how to live as those who have been justified by God's grace.[3]

And if the inner struggle for greater Christ-likeness is one aspect of Christian commitment, another is the battle against the external forces of the enemies of the gospel.

Paul's conversion certainly did not result in an easy life for him—far from it. He would tell young Timothy that Christianity means fighting a good fight (1 Tim. 1:18). He would speak to the believers of Lystra, Iconium and Antioch about entering the kingdom of God through many tribulations, (Acts 14:22) and so far as his own experience is concerned, he could list some of the sufferings he endured while in Christ's service:

> ... imprisonments, with countless beatings, and often near death. Five times I received at the hands of the Jews the forty lashes less one. Three times I was beaten with rods. Once I was stoned. Three times I was shipwrecked; for a night and a day I was adrift at sea; on frequent journeys, in danger from rivers, danger from robbers, danger from my own people, danger from Gentiles, danger in the city, danger in the wilderness, danger at sea, danger from false brothers; in toil and hardship, through many a sleepless night, in hunger and thirst, often without food, in cold and exposure (2 Cor. 11:23-27).

Such things, along with 'the pressure ... of my anxiety for all the churches' (2 Cor. 11:28), meant that Paul had a far from easy life.

Yet it was, in his estimation, a wonderful life and underneath everything there was a heart that exulted in the amazing grace of the Lord; as he would write, 'The life I now live in the flesh I

---

[3] In *The True Bounds of Christian Freedom* (Edinburgh: Banner of Truth, 1964), 72 (originally published 1645).

live by faith in the Son of God, who loved me and gave himself for me' (Gal. 2:20)—so that even if it should be in a miserable prison in Philippi, having been beaten and flogged, with his feet in the stocks, he (and Silas) would sing praises to God (Acts 16:25). Many people would have been moaning and cursing; they were singing hymns to God.

For Paul, the one-time enemy of the gospel, Christianity was not simply a philosophy of life, an ethical code or a new religion. It was all about a faith relationship with a living Lord—faith in the Son of God who loved *me*, he would say, and gave himself *for me* (Gal. 2:20).

A new way of thinking

Paul's conversion also resulted in a new way of thinking. Once he regarded Christianity as a wicked delusion and Christ as a blasphemer whose name and cause should be wiped out. Afterwards, he saw Christianity as the vital message that the world needed to hear, and Christ as the Saviour and Lord who wanted to bring abundant life (John 10:10) and eternal life (John 3:16).

That changed way of thinking is reflected well in 2 Corinthians 5:16: 'From now on, therefore, we regard no one according to the flesh. Even though we once regarded Christ according to the flesh, we regard him thus no longer.' This verse encapsulates his new way of thinking about other people and about Christ. He would no longer think of either in purely materialistic and this-worldly terms, as if this life is all that there is.

In the days of the Soviet Union, a European visitor to Leningrad consulted a map of the city. He noticed that, although he could see several church buildings from where he stood, they were not marked on the map. A passer-by explained, 'We don't show churches on our maps.' When the visitor said that there was *one* shown on the map, the Russian explained, 'That's now a museum, not a living church; it's only the living churches that we don't show'!

How sad an attitude is that, but it may be taken as a parable of a way of thinking that blots out certain factors, the kind of 'map' increasingly being given to young people in the West, in which the only things shown concern life in his world ('under the sun,' as the book of Ecclesiastes puts it), as if the pursuit of wealth, success, pleasure and power is all that matters.

Paul had been delivered from such a 'this-worldly' attitude, seeing everything rather in the light of eternity. The words already noted from 1 Timothy 1:15 reveal more of this changed outlook. Instead of seeing Jesus as a blasphemer and an enemy, Paul now spoke of a trustworthy saying—that 'Christ Jesus came into the world to save sinners, of whom I am the foremost.' In that short phrase Paul gives us the *who*, the *what*, the *why* and the *for whom* of the gospel:

- *Who?* For Paul, bringing together the two words 'Christ Jesus' was a profound thing. As a Jew, he had been look-ing forward to the coming of the Messiah, and 'Christ' is the Greek equivalent of that word. Most of his compatriots would not accept the remotest possibility that Jesus of Naz-areth could be the Messiah, and in Romans 9-11 he agonised over that sad fact. Yet at one time he too had hated the very thought—he couldn't stand it when these ridiculous Chris-tians talked about Jesus as the Messiah. Then his eyes were opened and he could speak of 'Christ Jesus.'

- *What* he did: he came into the world. He did not remain aloof in his heaven, but came right into this world with all its glory and grandeur on the one hand, and with all its sin and need on the other hand. The gospel is about One who was prepared (so to speak) to get his hands dirty—but more than that, to get his hands pierced.

- *Why* did he come? 'Christ Jesus came into the world to save.' Of course he came to do other things—to teach, to heal, to demonstrate a life of love, to challenge prejudice and injustice; but above all he came to save. 'God did not send his Son into the world to condemn the world, but in order that the world might be saved through him' (John 3:17).

- And *for whom?* He came 'to save sinners'—which is good news for us as sinners in need of his forgiving grace and salvation. Paul describes himself as the foremost sinner (1 Tim 1:15). And if we ask whether this could be fake humility, the answer is that Paul's writings reveal the heartfelt worship and gratitude of someone who realised his own unworthiness and who could pre-date the famous words of the renowned Sir James Young Simpson (discoverer of the anaesthetic powers of chloroform) when he was asked what was his *greatest* discovery and answered, 'That I am great sinner and Jesus Christ is a great Saviour.'

While considering Paul's new way of thinking, we should perhaps refer to the idea suggested by some people that Paul *changed* Christianity and that we have to get behind his so-called theologising to the essentially simple message of Jesus, who (it is sometimes implied by those who say such things) went around telling nice stories and encouraging us all to be nice to each other.

People have been known to say of some text or other from the epistles, 'Ah but that was only Paul'—as if to say that his teaching is less significant than the words of Jesus—the impression given inadvertently by those red-letter Bibles which print the words of Jesus in red letters to make them stand out. Of course the words of Jesus are precious, but Christian belief is that the whole Bible is God's inspired word and is profitable for us (2 Tim. 3:16); that includes the words of the apostle Paul. We may summarise the point in some words of James S. Stewart on such attempts to drive a wedge between Jesus and Paul:

> The truth is that all the apostle's great central conceptions— the grace of God, the justifying of the sinner, the adoption of sons, the death of the Redeemer and all the rest—came to him straight out of the bosom of Jesus' gospel. Jesus himself inspired every one of them. It is repeatedly stated that… what we call Christianity today bears Paul's signature more clearly than Christ's. A gulf indeed there was. How could there fail to be a gulf, when One was the Redeemer and the other the redeemed? But between the Gospel which Jesus brought by his life and teaching and death and resurrection—and the Gospel which Paul in season and out of season proclaimed, there was no gulf at all.[4]

Someone has referred to bookshops where the 'religion' section has a new shelf—'Books for Angry Unbelievers'—books by, among others, Richard Dawkins, Sam Harris and the late Christopher Hitchens. The Paul portrayed in the New Testament would once have been happy to be numbered among them— angry unbelievers. Once upon a time unbelievers were generally tolerant and accepting of the fact that many people do seriously and sincerely believe in God, but now these so-called 'new atheists' are (if we can contort language slightly) evangelistic atheists. I say 'contort language' because, of course, 'evangel' means good news, and there isn't any good news in atheism.

---

[4] James S. Stewart, *A Man in Christ* (London: Hodder & Stoughton, 1935), 18f.

At the time of writing, there is great concern in the UK about the growing amount of knife crime, sexual assault, and gambling addiction. Public entertainment majors on profanity and immorality, and politicians have taken it on themselves to 'redefine' marriage and indoctrinate the minds of very young children about gender choices, different kinds of families, and tolerance—although tolerance has for many people come to mean *in*tolerance of anyone who disagrees with what is deemed to be politically correct. A British Member of Parliament has written,

> Religious believers are, once again, facing increased pressure to restrict their faith to the 'private sphere.' We now see regular and increasingly unapologetic persecution of Christians who remain committed to Biblical teaching, refusing to bow to liberal, secular orthodoxies. Although it is now Bible-believing Christians who face increasing discrimination today, radical secularists are every bit as determined to undermine the freedoms of observant Muslims and orthodox Jews.[5]

Through his conversion Paul gained a new way of thinking, in which everything was related to God's will for the world. He himself had become a new creation in Christ (2 Cor. 5:17) and he longed for other people to find salvation and peace through the gospel.

A new mission

Besides having a new life and a new way of thinking, Paul also had a new mission. Not only was the former enemy now a believer but he was someone who had in his heart and mind a passionate desire to tell others. He had found good news and it was too good to keep to himself. What happened on the Damascus Road was not only a turning point in Paul's own life but also in the

[5] Sir John Hayes MP; quoted in *Barnabas Prayer*, March/April 2019.

mission of the church. Much of the book of Acts tells of his energetic and costly efforts to spread the gospel; it could be said (at that human level) that it is through his work and ministry that we have had the gospel message handed on to us.

The latter part of the book of Acts, along with the letters of Paul, give us the testimony of one who had been one of the fiercest critics of Christianity and one of the most resolute enemies of Christ. We referred earlier to his words in 1 Corinthians 15:9, 'I persecuted the church of God.' He regarded himself as unworthy to be an apostle because of that, but he went on, 'But by the grace of God I am what I am, and his grace towards me was not in vain. On the contrary, I worked harder than any of them, though it was not I, but the grace of God that is with me' (1 Cor. 15:10).

So it is that we find him saying in Acts 20:24, 'I do not account my life of any value… if only I may … testify to the gospel of the grace of God.' That is some transformation! Enemies of Christ can, by the grace of God, become his friends, his children, and his servants. Then we can join with those who rejoice in this great gospel and sing:

> How marvellous! How wonderful!
> and my song shall ever be:
> How marvellous! How wonderful
> Is my Saviour's love for me![6]

---

[6] Hymn by Charles Hutchinson Gabriel (1856–1932).

8

What's in a Name?

What's in a name? It's a famous question, asked by Juliet in Shakespeare's *Romeo and Juliet*. She went on, 'That which we call a rose by any other name would smell as sweet,'[1] and that's true. If the flower we know as a rose had happened to be called a turnip, it would still have the same sweet fragrance and it would still look as beautiful. In the play, Romeo might be a Montague, while Juliet belonged to the rival Capulet family, but she wasn't in love with his name but with *him* as a person.

However, there *is* sometimes a great deal in a name, especially in biblical times. We might think of Jesus giving Simon the name Peter (Rock) to signify the foundational nature of the faith that Peter had expressed (Matt. 16:18), and of course there is the angelic message to Joseph that said, 'You shall call his name Jesus [which means Saviour] for he will save his people from their sins' (Matt. 1:21).

In Acts 11:26 Luke gives the simple statement, 'In Antioch the disciples were first called Christians.' He doesn't specifically tell us that the name was given by people who were *enemies* of Christ, but they probably were not themselves believers; they were presumably ordinary observers of what was going on in the town.

[1] *Romeo And Juliet*, Act 2, Scene 2, lines 43-44.

I suppose it is possible that it was the disciples themselves who invented the term. Verse 21 tells us that a great number of people turned to the Lord, and verse 24 similarly says, 'A great many people were added to the Lord' and perhaps these converts coined the new term themselves.

But the simplest interpretation of Luke's words is that the name came from the people of Antioch—whether enemies of Christ or perhaps simply ordinary Antiochenes who were making a neutral comment. Whether it was used dismissively ('these Christ people') or with a kind of reluctant admiration, it is remarkable that the name which has come to be the standard name for Christ's people through the centuries started out as a sort of nickname.

Most people would assume that the word *Christian* is to be found all over the New Testament, and would be surprised to know that it was not in fact the normal word for Jesus' followers. The normal word was 'saints', although used in a different sense from its current popular usage—not describing particularly holy or 'religious' people, but sinners who were being sanctified through the work of the Holy Spirit.

The word is found some sixty times in the New Testament, whereas the word Christian is only found thrice: apart from Acts 11:26, it is found in Acts 26:28, where it is used sarcastically by King Agrippa ('next you'll be making a Christian of me!') and in 1 Peter 4:15-16: 'Let none of you suffer as a murderer or a thief or an evildoer or as a meddler. Yet if anyone suffers as a Christian, let him not be ashamed but let him glorify God in that name.'

The origin of the name

Antioch was a large and strategic city of the Roman empire, a cosmopolitan place of about half a million souls; in the Roman world, only Rome itself and Alexandria were larger. If the gospel could be established in that city, it would be a significant thing in itself and for the people of Antioch, and it would also make a strategic base for further advance.

Luke tells us that the martyrdom of Stephen marked the beginning of a period of persecution, leading to a scattering of believers, some of whom came to Antioch. Not for the last time, a time of persecution became the springboard for further gospel advance. As would be said later, the blood of martyrs was seed for the church.[2]

Stoning must have been a terrible way to die—yet the record says (Acts 7:55), 'But he, full of the Holy Spirit, gazed into heaven and saw the glory of God, and Jesus standing at the right hand of God.' And as they hurled rocks on him, he 'called out, "Lord Jesus, receive my spirit." And falling to his knees he cried out with a loud voice, "Lord, do not hold this sin again them." And when he had said this, he fell asleep' (Acts 7:59-60). It was so like the Master in whose name he was being martyred (Luke 23:34).

This was the first Christian martyrdom and perhaps it came as a big shock to some believers; if any Christian had believed that following Jesus would lead to an easy life, or that the cause of Christ was going to take over the world within a few months, this event would have shattered such illusions. To see such a stalwart as Stephen being stoned to death may have troubled some people.

Acts 8 goes on to say, 'There arose on that day a great persecution against the church in Jerusalem, and they were all scattered throughout the regions of Judea and Samaria, except the apostles' (Acts 8:1). It would have seemed to many to be a strange

---

[2] Tertullian in his second century *Apology,* chapter 50.13.

providence, but it was through this scattering that the Holy Spirit led the church in the fulfilment of what the risen Lord had said in Acts 1:8: 'You will be my witnesses in Jerusalem and in all Judea and Samaria and to the end of the earth.'

And *in* Antioch a remarkable thing happened, something that could easily slip by us because it seems so obvious now—some people preached the gospel to gentiles.

Chapters ten and eleven of Acts tell of the conversion of the Roman centurion Cornelius, and there was a gradual realisation that Christianity was not just a Jewish sect; the gospel was for all nations and races. When the believers came to Antioch, verse nineteen of Acts 11 says that initially they spoke the word to the Jews only, but some others spoke to the Hellenists (Greek-speaking gentiles) also, 'preaching the Lord Jesus. And the hand of the Lord was with them, and a great number who believed turned to the Lord' (Acts 11:20-21).

So, the martyrdom of Stephen and the subsequent persecution of the church, dreadful as these events were, resulted, under the over-ruling providence of God, in this remarkable forward move for the gospel.

Verse twenty described them as 'preaching' and the Greek word has *evangel* at its heart—they *good-newsed* about Jesus—because the gospel is just that: it is good news. It is not good advice about how we ought to live, but good news about what God has done for us through the incarnation, teaching, death and resurrection of Christ.

When the Jerusalem church learned that amazing things were happening up north in Antioch, they thought it good to send someone to encourage them and they made the inspired choice of Barnabas, one of the great figures of the early days.

The New International Version expands the English Standard Version's 'he came and saw the grace of God' (Acts 11:23) to read, 'He arrived and saw the evidence of the grace of God.' The evidence was that of the gospel not only convincing Jews to put their trust in Jesus as their Messiah but also convincing gentiles to turn from their sin and put their trust in Christ. And just as Peter found (Acts 10 and 11) that he couldn't argue with what God was clearly doing, so Barnabas in Antioch realised that there was something bigger going on than any of them had anticipated.

The other thing that Barnabas did was to send for Saul, and verses twenty-five and twenty-six of Acts 11 must be among the most significant verses in the New Testament: 'Barnabas went to Tarsus to look for Saul, and when he had found him, he brought him to Antioch. For a whole year they met with the church and taught a great many people.'

Barnabas realised that help was needed, and to whom did he turn but to Saul of Tarsus. Of course this Saul became Paul the apostle, the apostle to the gentiles, a man who would spend his great energy for the advance of the gospel in the ensuing years, starting from Antioch as the base for his famous missionary journeys. Something like nine years had elapsed since Saul's own encounter with the risen Christ on the road to Damascus (Acts 9) and now he was ready to embark on what was to be his life's work.

And it is at this point that Luke, the author of Acts, informs us of the use of the term 'Christian'. As we have noted, 'Christian' seems to have started as a nickname. Antioch was apparently a great place for nicknames—when the emperor Julian visited Antioch, for example, and people saw his little beard, they nicknamed him *'the Goat'*!

There were other names for the followers of the Lord. Acts 2:27 calls them 'those who were being saved;' Acts 6:1 describes them as 'disciples;' in Acts 9:13, when Ananias was told to go to see Saul, he protested, 'Lord, I have heard from many about this man, how much evil he has done to your saints at Jerusalem.' Other names include 'the brothers' (9:30), 'the believers' (5:14) and 'the Nazarenes' (24:5). However, 'Christians' became the name used through the centuries for the followers of the Lord, and it would perhaps surprise many people to know that the name was possibly fastened on them by other people.

The aptness of the name 'Christian'

It is surely significant that 'Christian' was the name given by the people of Antioch. Antioch named these people by what they saw in, and heard from them, and the main thing that they saw and heard was not a code of morality or a set of new religious rituals. It was not just a new 'religion,' although of course the Christian religion was to outlive all of the proud and seemingly invincible emperors who held sway then—a point made once by the late Richard Bewes when he said that these emperors could never have imagined that, twenty centuries later, people would name their children after the followers of Jesus (for example, John, Thomas, Andrew), while their names (Caesar, Nero) would be reserved for their household pets![3]

The people of Antioch didn't see simply a new religion, but people who belonged to Jesus, people who worshipped and loved Jesus, people who served Jesus and sought to introduce others to him. What was said of the Scottish preacher John Duncan could have been said of the Christians of Antioch also:

[3] Richard Bewes (1934–2019), minister of All Souls Church in London, speaking at a 'Prom Praise' concert in Edinburgh, August 1993.

Jesus Christ, in His person, His character, His life, His death, was the central subject of his thoughts, and increasingly year by year till the end. It was not theology but Christ that filled both his mind and his heart; the whole stream of his theology sprang from Him as its source and flowed to Him as its ocean.[4]

They spoke about Jesus in words, and we can be sure also that 'the disciples were called Christians' because there was something of Christ evident in their lives. The giving of the name speaks of the witness they bore, both by their words and by their lives. For them, Jesus was not simply an inspiring example from the past or a great teacher who had gone bravely to a horrible death. Rather Jesus was everything to them—their Saviour, their Redeemer, their Lord and Master, their Friend, their Guide; he was their strength in testing times and their hope for future times; in everything, Christ was the centre: in their faith, their worship, their prayer, their fellowship, their lives, their witness.

One of the summer jobs I had as a student was in a department store in Edinburgh and there was a member of staff there who was Polish by nationality. His name was Mr Kunicki (everyone in those days was known by titles rather than first-names) and he would sometimes object to something that another employee had said. The other was a professing Christian and Mr Kunicki would say, 'You should love other people; you are a Jesus Christ man.'

In Antioch the believers were recognised as Jesus Christ people; that's why the term *Christian* was coined to describe them. Whether the originators of the name were actual enemies of Christ or simply neutral observers, it was gospel truth. To be a

---

[4] A. Moody Stuart, *Recollections of the late John Duncan* (Edinburgh: Edmonston & Douglas, 1872), 166.

follower of Jesus means to be a Jesus Christ person. It is the most apt name possible.

The challenge of the name

Clearly the challenge that comes from the choice of such a name is: if the people of our time and our locality were asked to invent a name for those who follow Christ, what would it be?

Would they call us *church-goers*? That is a fair possibility and it would be reasonable because obviously Christians go to church.

They might derisively refer to *Bible bashers*—and it is true that we would want to be known as people who believe the Bible and seek to live by it, but we don't want to be known as people who try to push things down other people's throats.

Fundamentalists is another possibility—another term that may have a good sense if it means standing on the fundamentals, but we all know it has come to be used as a synonym for extremist.

How good it would be if the term they would choose would be *Christian*—in other words, if there was something about the lives and characters of God's people that speaks of Christ, something (in the words of the old chorus) of the beauty of Jesus being seen in us.

Some years ago a Christian magazine told a story from the then Soviet Union about a criminal called Koslov who had been imprisoned but who later became a Christian and, later still, a church leader. He looked back on his time in prison and the example of some fellow-prisoners in whom he had seen something of the beauty and compassion of Jesus:

> Among the general despair, while prisoners like myself were cursing ourselves, the camp, the authorities, while we opened up our veins or our stomachs, or hanged ourselves, the Christians (often with sentences of 20 to 25 years) did not despair.

One could see Christ reflected in their faces, their pure, upright life, deep faith and devotion to God. Their gentleness and their wonderful manliness became a shining example of real life for thousands.[5]

They were apparently people of whom it might be said that their fellow-prisoners recognised them as Christians, even there in prison.

Catherine Booth who, with her husband William, founded the Salvation Army, said:

> There are teeming thousands who never cross the threshold of church, chapel or mission hall, to whom all connected with religion is an old song, a byword and a reproach. They need to be brought into contact with a living Christ in the characters and persons of his people.

Although these words were spoken a long time ago, they remain relevant, especially in a time when fewer and fewer people attend any place of worship: 'They need to be brought into contact with a living Christ in the characters and persons of his people.'[6]

Such is the challenge of the name Christian, given by people who were observers of what was happening. Whether they were outright enemies or not, they got it right when they realised that the best name for followers of Jesus Christ is *Christians*.

[5] *Christianity Today*, 21 June 1974.
[6] Catherine Bramwell-Booth, *Catherine Booth* (London: Hodder Christian Paperbacks, 1973), 310.

9

Upside Down Kingdom

During Paul's second missionary journey, he and Silas came to Thessalonica. Acts 17:2-3 says that he followed his usual custom of going first to the local Jewish synagogue and 'on three Sabbath days he reasoned with them from the Scriptures, explaining and proving that it was necessary for the Christ to suffer and to rise from the dead, and saying, "This Jesus, whom I proclaim to you, is the Christ."'

Some listeners were converted but others reacted very negatively. Some people stirred up a disturbance and when they couldn't find Paul and Silas, they seized the hospitable Jason who had 'received' the missionaries. They brought him before the city authorities and asserted that he had welcomed certain undesirables, men who were turning the world upside down in allegiance to another king, namely Jesus.

This is another instance of the gospel according to Christ's enemies. It is true—these men *were* turning the world upside down and they *were* advocating allegiance to King Jesus.

Of course, the apostles would have made the point that it wasn't they who were causing this upheaval but their Master, the living Lord Jesus Christ; they would also have said that it was really a case of turning an upside down world right-side-up! In so many ways, the world then was upside down in its reckoning (just as we could say it is today also).

Christ's enemies meant it as an accusation but it is an accurate description of the impact of the gospel—as expressed elsewhere when Paul wrote, 'If anyone is in Christ he is a new creation' (2 Cor. 5:17).

The New International Version translates the allegation of these enemies of the gospel as: 'These men who have caused trouble all over the world…' The Greek word signifies upsetting or destabilising, and the accusation that Paul and Silas were 'acting against the decrees of Caesar and saying that there is another king, Jesus' (Acts 17:7) was presumably meant to ring alarm bells in the minds of the authorities.

Wasn't it the tactic used by Jesus' enemies at his trial—they alleged that he was politically dangerous, a threat to the ruling power, Rome. And wasn't it the voice that said, 'If you let this man go, you are no friend of Caesar' (John 19:12) that sent chills down the spine of Pontius Pilate and led that weak governor to finally sign the death warrant?

What a contrast it is to the view that Christianity is a mild and anodyne philosophy that causes the minimum of upheaval, along with the idea that Jesus was a rather unworldly, ethereal sort-of figure who has a vague influence on people in the sense of moving them to 'be nice to each other.'

True Christianity turns the world upside down, and if ever a society needed Acts 17:6 it is our Western secular society. A friend of mine drew attention to a comment in an article in the French magazine *Le Figaro:* 'The secularist drive to rid France of its Christian past is becoming insane'; that is true of Western society generally as many people try to re-write history and write Christianity out of public life.

Radical change

Consider this question posed by an evangelist: who was the greatest revolutionary who ever lived? Would it be perhaps Karl Marx, or one of his followers who stood one day in his town square making a fiery speech about the need for revolutionary change in his country. He said, 'Those of you who are prepared to give your lives that a revolution might take place, I call you to step out of the crowd and join me.' A grand total of seventeen stepped forward, but that man, Vladimir Ilyich Lenin, convinced others, and soon it was 17,000 people, and so on and so on until the revolution convulsed Russia and part of Europe for much of the twentieth century.

Someone else has suggested, rather more whimsically perhaps, that the greatest revolutionary could be Henry Ford. In the early days when he was producing and promoting the motor car, there were doctors who said that speeding along at 10mph was more than the human heart could stand, and when the speed increased to a fantastic 30mph they said, 'The human body will never be able to take it; get it off the road!'

However, the conclusion of the evangelist who posed the question was: 'Of all the men who walked the face of the earth to bring about true radical change, Jesus Christ, God's Son, the man from heaven, was the greatest revolutionary who ever lived.'[1] Is that exaggeration, an evangelist's rhetoric, or is it sober truth— that Jesus has caused more radical change and revolution in the world than anyone else—that he has, in the words of Acts 17:6, 'turned the world upside down'?

[1] Tom Skinner, *Black & Free* (Grand Rapids: Zondervan, 1969).

It's what had happened in Paul's own case. In Philippians he wrote about the great change that came about in his life because of what happened on the Road to Damascus. Everything changed in his heart and mind, so that he could write, 'Whatever gain I had, I counted as loss for the sake of Christ. Indeed, I count everything as loss because of the surpassing worth of knowing Christ Jesus my Lord' (Phil. 3:7-8).

These Thessalonian enemies of Christianity and Christ were saying something that was wonderfully true without realising it. These Christians—or rather the gospel and Christ whom they preached as a living reality—were indeed turning things and people upside down. If that is causing trouble, let there be more and more of it!

One is reminded of the saying of King George II about General Wolfe's campaigns in Canada. The Duke of Newcastle was an opponent of William Pitt's handling of the war and he advocated peace at any cost. Just before Wolfe took Quebec in September 1759, the Duke said that this particular Wolfe was going mad. The King responded, 'Mad, is he? Then I wish he would bite some of my other generals!'[2]

If we look back to the chapter 16 of Acts, we see something of this revolutionary impact of the gospel in the stories of the three remarkably diverse converts in Philippi. First there was a poor slave-girl who had some kind of religious mania and kept following Paul around and shouting out things about these men being servants of the true God. What she was saying was true, but the manner of it was not helpful. Paul realised that there was something wrong with her, and in the name and by the power

---

[2] From title page of *Mad, Is He?—the Character and Achievement of James Wolfe* by D. Grinnell-Milne (London: Bodley Head, 1963).

of Christ he restored her to sanity and peace of mind. Is that causing trouble?

Just before that there was Lydia, a woman from the other end of the social scale, a successful businesswoman. She heard the gospel from Paul, and she was wonderfully converted, no doubt finding new meaning and fulfilment in her life, including in her religious life.

And thirdly, in Philippi there was the jailor who was about to take his own life because he thought that his prisoners had escaped and that he would be in serious trouble. His life too was turned around completely and, instead of taking his own life, he started bathing his prisoners' wounds after midnight in the ruins of the earthquake-shaken prison. Here was another man—in fact, another family—wonderfully turned from darkness to light and from the power of evil to the love of Christ. Is that causing trouble? If it is, may there be more trouble.

What was true then has been true through the centuries. Where the gospel has gone, it has made a difference, notably bringing the twin blessings of education and healthcare in its train—is that causing trouble? Today—where there are Christian workers bringing education to people who cannot afford to pay for it, where there are Christian medics working in poorly-equipped hospitals for salaries that are paltry compared with what they would receive if employed by the National Health Service, where there are people in the name of Christ seeking to reclaim lives from addiction to drugs and alcohol, where there are people digging wells and spreading agricultural know-how—if such things amount to causing trouble, let's have more of it!

This passage in Acts 17 speaks of a world that is upside down and a gospel that is revolutionary in its effects.

Upside down world

Many examples of 'upside-down-ness' could be given. We might reflect, for example, on the salaries that are paid to sporting stars, entertainers, broadcasters and others (one famous foot-baller receives £28m a year), while people like the much admired fire-fighters who sometimes risk their own lives for other people, receive an average of something like £32,000. Football is a fine game and an engaging (not to say addictive) pastime, but isn't that disparity a clear indication of the upside down scale of values in the modern world?

Back in 2015, the three leading cinema chains in the UK refused to screen a sixty second advert which featured the Lord's Prayer. The advert was cleared by the Cinema Advertising Authority and the British Board of Film Classification, but the Odeon, Cine-world and Vue chains (which together cover 80% of British cin-emas) refused to show it because it carried 'the risk of upsetting or offending audiences'[3]—a decision described in *The Guardian* as 'nonsense on stilts.'

What makes the matter a case of upside-down-ness is the fact that, while banning that sixty-second advert, the same cinemas regularly screen films that include profanity, blasphemy, extreme violence and all manner of scenes that could be said to run the risk of 'upsetting or offending audiences.'

At another level, our parliaments have spent much time debating and eventually banning hunting with dogs, a decision that is surely welcomed by many people; yet at the same time our laws allow for the tearing apart of babies in the womb, often on trivial grounds (about nine and a half million since the 1967 Abortion Act).

[3] Giles Fraser in *The Guardian*, 22 November 2015.

Other examples could be given of ways in which this is a topsy-turvy world with inverted values.

A revolutionary gospel

If the passage in Acts 17 speaks about an upside down world, it also speaks about a revolutionary gospel, a message that really makes a difference. There in Thessalonica it was turning things upside down—as the enemies of the gospel put it. From their lips that was an accusation and a criticism, but from the Bible's point of view it is wonderfully true—except that, as we have suggested, Paul would have said, 'No, not upside down—right-side-up.'

Christianity is not a tame little message that amounts to little more than 'be nice to each other.' The socialist economist R. H. Tawney recognised that almost a hundred years ago when he wrote, 'To state that the social ethics of the New Testament are obligatory on men in the business affairs which occupy nine-tenths of their thought, or on the industrial organisation that gives our society its character, is to preach revolution.'[4] How sad that so often the Christian message has been toned down, reduced to a kind of prudential morality and inoffensive message that makes little difference to anything.

Think of some of the revolutionary things the Bible says:

- Proverbs 1:7 says, 'The fear of the Lord is the beginning of wisdom'—which is very different from the attitude of our upside down world in which so many people have no fear or respect for God.

- In the letter of James we read, 'Count it all joy when you meet trials of various kinds' (James 1:2). That also turns the values of the world upside down, seeing troubles not

[4] R. H. Tawney, *The Acquisitive Society* (London: Collins, 1921), 180.

as frustrating things that inevitably spoil life but as opportunities for growth in character.

- Ecclesiastes 12:1 says, 'Remember your Creator in the days of your youth.' An upside down world has no time for that and more often encourages the young to forget any notions of even the existence of a Creator, much less of adherence to his standards and values.

Or think of the kind of things Jesus said:

- In Matthew 19:4 we read, 'He who created them from the beginning made them male and female, and said, "Therefore a man shall leave his father and his mother and hold fast to his wife."' The world has tried to turn that upside down, with our parliaments thinking they have the right to 're-define' marriage, as if it belonged to them to do so, and currently campaigns are going on to challenge the very concepts of maleness and femaleness, to the confusion of the minds of even very young children.

- And what about: 'If anyone would come after me, let him deny himself, take up his cross and follow me' (Mark 8:34). The world is more interested in self-expression, self-promotion, self-assertion and self-esteem—anything rather than self-denial.

- Deuteronomy 8:3 says, 'Man does not live by bread alone,' a saying which challenges the attitudes of this materialistic world in which so many people are motivated by the desire for more and more things. In the rules for the game of Monopoly, various things are explained before it simply says that at the end of the game the player with the most money is the winner. That may be fine for a board game, but it is no way to live in the real world. Paul wrote about people whose greatest desire is to be rich—'It is through this craving that some have wandered away from the faith' (1 Tim. 6:10). He said that we shouldn't set our hopes on 'the uncertainty of riches, but on God, who richly provides us with everything to enjoy' (verse 17).

These passages (and others that could be cited) reveal the truly radical nature of the Bible's claims; they testify to the truth of the charge made by the enemies of Christ that his gospel does indeed turn the world upside down.

When I was an undergraduate in Edinburgh, Malcolm Muggeridge was Rector of the University, and when students expected him to represent and pursue their demands for the free availability of contraceptive pills, he resigned. In a famous sermon in Edinburgh, he spoke of having what he called 'a twentieth century sceptical mind and sensual disposition' and characterised society as holding:

> …a strange mixture of crazy credulity in certain directions, as for instance in science and advertising … and equally crazy scepticism, so that illiterate schoolboys and half-baked university students turn aside with contemptuous disbelief before propositions which the greatest minds and the noblest dispositions of our civilisation—Pascal say, and Tolstoy—accepted as self-evident. That is our twentieth century plight.[5]

How much more is this true of the message contained in Scripture, the message inspired by God and profitable for human beings (2 Tim. 3:16, 17). The truth is that, far from causing trouble and destabilising the world, the message of the Bible is what our world desperately needs; it is that which can bring stability to the world.

[5] Malcolm Muggeridge, *Another King* (Edinburgh: Saint Andrew Press, 1968), 7.

Its revolutionary turning of things right-side-up relates to both a new way of salvation and a new way of living.

A new way of salvation

In the first place, the message of the Bible speaks of a new way of salvation. It was a basic belief of other religions, and it remains the religion of most people, that there are certain things one has to do in order to be in good standing with God; if people do so many good deeds or say so many prayers, then God will hopefully accept them.

In one of his books, the evangelist Michael Green tells of finding a gravestone in an ancient church:

> It enshrined superbly this idea that I do my best and God ought to be very pleased with it, and it shows how repulsive that idea really is. It comes from King Ethelred the Unready, and it runs like this: 'I, Ethelred, king of Albion, in order that on the awful day of judgment I may, by the intercession of the saints, be deemed worthy to be admitted to the heavenly kingdom, do give Almighty God the possession of three lands (farms) to be held for ever for the monastery of the aforesaid martyr'.[6]

The story is told in a book called *You Must Be Joking!* Unfortunately, many people are not joking when they pin their hopes on such self-salvation. The Bible turns the idea of self-salvation upside down. It tells us that there is no way we could ever be saved by such means, but that *God* has acted for the salvation of the world.

In Acts 17, Luke only gives a brief summary of the message that was preached by Paul in Thessalonica. Verse 2 tells of him speaking in the synagogues, 'reasoning with them from the Scriptures,

[6] Michael Green, *You Must Be Joking* (London: Hodder & Stoughton, 1976), 97.

explaining and proving' the necessity of Christ's sufferings and death to save his people.

Paul saw himself as a herald, someone sent to announce a message, whether people liked it or not. That didn't mean that he simply shouted it loudly without engaging his hearers; in fact, we find him using every means of persuading them 'that the Christ had to suffer and rise from the dead,' and then saying, 'This Jesus, whom I proclaim to you, is the Christ.'

That's as much as Luke records on that occasion, but even that short excerpt lets us realise that Paul's message centred in Jesus Christ—Jesus Christ crucified and risen.

When he referred to the necessity of Christ's passion, he pointed to the heart of the Bible's message of atonement. The reason why Jesus 'had to' suffer and die was not the weakness of Pontius Pilate, the machinations of the Jewish leaders, the betrayal of Judas or any other human factor. The necessity relates to *God*'s purpose, the fulfilment of his word that One would come to take mankind's sin in himself and accept the Father's wrath against sin in himself for the salvation of all who will accept it from his hand.

That way of salvation is a gospel; it is good news, not of what we have to do but of what God in Christ has done for us.

The centre of the gospel is Jesus himself, and here we find the enemies of the gospel recognising that. Their accusation was, 'They are acting against the decrees of Caesar and saying that there is another king, Jesus.' Christianity is not principally about the teaching or example of Jesus. It is about Jesus Christ himself, in all the glory of his person as the Son of Man and Son of God, bringing salvation as his free gift.

In the other religions of the time, including emperor-worship, there was little personal commitment. It didn't matter whether you even believed that the gods existed, so long as you went through the outward rituals. It was and is different with Christianity, which is all about personal commitment to the person of Jesus Christ as Saviour and King.

This is what the enemies of the gospel in Thessalonica recognised—it's all about allegiance to another King, Jesus. They recognised a revolutionary gospel when they saw one.

A new way of living

And if the gospel turns things upside down in its revelation of a new way of salvation, it is also revolutionary in terms of a new way of living.

This new way of living was notable in the first century when Christians were living out their faith against the background of paganism with all kinds of immorality—they were turning the world upside down with their talk of costly, sacrificial love to other people, even loving your enemies (Matt. 5:44); being faithful to one spouse in marriage (Heb. 13:4); turning the other cheek (Matt. 5:39); visiting orphans and widows in their affliction (James 1:27).

The members of that early church had a new scale of values, a new view of what are the most important things in life. They thought less of money and possessions; they believed it is more blessed to give than to receive (Acts 20:35). They not only read the Scriptures but enjoyed doing so; prayer became a powerful reality to them, and Luke gives the following cameo picture of the vitality of Christian living in the early church:

> They devoted themselves to the apostles' teaching and the fellowship, to the breaking of bread and the prayers. And awe came upon every soul, and many wonders and signs were being done through the apostles. And all who believed were together

and had all things in common, and they were selling their possessions and belongings and distributing the proceeds to all, as any had need. And day by day, attending the temple together and breaking bread in their homes, they received their food with glad and generous hearts, praising God and having favour with all the people And the Lord added to their number day by day those who were being saved. (Acts 2:42-47)

The long and short of it was that Jesus was the most important thing (Person) in life to them, and we know that, if necessary, they were prepared to suffer and die for him and his Kingdom. For, of course, the phrase in the passage quoted above about having favour with the people didn't remain universally true. Many turned against them and times of persecution soon came (and continue to this day in many parts of the world).

We live in a world very different from the world of first century Thessalonica, but it is still Christ's call to live out our faith and commitment, demonstrating this radical message that really does make a difference. Paul's words, 'If anyone is in Christ, he is a new creation,' (2 Cor. 5:17) point to a truly radical change which has been expressed by someone who said, 'When I met Christ, it was as if lightning struck, knocking me conscious'!

It was his enemies who said it, but Jesus really does turn the world upside down; that's the gospel according to Christ's enemies. And if that's causing trouble, let's have a lot more trouble! Far from destabilising the world, this is the one thing that can turn the world right side up, bring stability, peace and fulfilment. It all centres in this other King, Jesus.

10

This Babbler!

Christianity has often been dismissed as just meaningless words, although few might go as far as Professor Richard Dawkins in describing religious belief as 'a virus of the mind.' He asks, 'What has theology ever said that is of the smallest use to anybody? The achievements of theologians don't do anything, don't affect anything, don't achieve anything, don't even mean anything.'[1]

Another of the so-called 'new atheists' has written, 'Surely there must come a time when we will acknowledge the obvious: theology is now little more than a branch of human ignorance.'[2]

Not many enemies of Christianity would be quite so virulent (and intolerant), although much of modern culture works with an assumption that 'religion' is *infra dig*, out of fashion, only fit to be relegated to the museum of *how things used to be*.

---

[1] Quotations given in John Blanchard, *Does God Believe in Atheists?* (Darlington: Evangelical Press, 2000), 190-91.

[2] Sam Harris, *The End of Faith* (London: The Free Press, 2005), 173. This is very different from the more restrained attitude of Brian Cox (Professor of Particle Physics at the University of Manchester) who has described science, philosophy, theology and religion as different ways of trying to come to terms with reality. When asked, 'How can you be sure there isn't a God?' he answered, 'I can't,' and said also, 'I think science is about being comfortable with answering questions with 'I don't know.' www.bbc.co.uk/programmes/p07br0zk (accessed 29 June 2019).

Whether explicitly stated or not, many atheists would dismiss people who try to speak to others about it as 'babblers'.

If that is so, at least we are in good company! Paul was evangelising in Athens and his strategy involved going to the synagogue to reason with the Jews, and to engage with people in the market place—where some dismissed him as nothing more than a mere babbler.

In ornithology a babbler is a songbird with a loud discordant voice! But the Greek word (*spermologos*) means a seed-picker and hence metaphorically someone who picks up bits and pieces of ideas from here, there and everywhere to make a religious hotchpotch. That, according to the intelligentsia of Athens, was Paul.

Were they actual enemies of Christ and Christianity? Perhaps not, but they were certainly dismissive of the preacher. Paul was waiting in Athens for the arrival of his colleagues Silas and Timothy, and we are told by Luke that while he waited for them, 'his spirit was provoked within him as he saw that the city was full of idols' (Acts 17:16).

Athens

One scholar has written, 'The Athens of this vivid story was in the late afternoon of her glory,'[3] but it was still one of the great cities of the ancient world, and Paul would not be blind to its cultural achievements. He could no doubt appreciate grand buildings, cultural creativity and philosophical debate.

But, for all the splendour and sense of history around him, there was something that brought great distress to his soul: the city was full of idols. Whatever might be said about the beauty of their construction, the tragedy was that people were worshipping

[3] E. M. Blaiklock, *Acts—An Introduction and Commentary* (Leicester: IVP, 1959), 132.

idols and knew nothing of Christ and his great salvation. That is what caused distress to the apostle.

- The Athenians had great architecture. There was the splendid Parthenon up on the Acropolis and many other buildings of great merit; there were statues and monuments, 'some of which have survived the incredible battering of twenty-three centuries and stand today, a monument to the worth of human effort when willing hands work as one under the inspiration of a grand idea.'[4] But they didn't have Christ.

- They had intellect: this had been the city of Plato and Aristotle, and its university was one of the three great universities of the world. But they didn't have Christ, and that's what distressed Paul.

- They had culture—famous dramatists and actors wrote and acted there; they had had Sophocles and Euripides. But they had no knowledge of Christ.

- Athens is regarded as the birthplace of democracy, which was part of its legacy to the world. But they didn't have Christ.

- They had a language (from which English has borrowed extensively) which has been described as 'perhaps the most perfect instrument of human expression in the history of speech;'[5] but they didn't have Christ.

Much of Athens' glory may have been in the past, but it was still a great city. Visitors then would often be impressed, even as

[4] Ibid, 133.
[5] Ibid, 133.

visitors today will marvel at the ancient ruins. But, whether Paul was impressed or not, we're told that he was distressed. 'His spirit was provoked within him as he saw that the city was full of idols' (Acts 17:16).

'New and strange ideas'

It was as he sought to proclaim the message of Christ that he was dismissed as a babbler[6] and proclaimer of novel and weird ideas (Acts 17:19, 20). And when he spoke about Jesus' resurrection, we are told that some scoffed, some put off any decision and a few became believers.

The people who dismissed him in this way are introduced as Epicurean and Stoic philosophers. The word *epicurean* is used now to describe the pursuit of sensual pleasures but originally Epicureanism sought contented tranquillity through detachment from material things. It was not necessarily atheistic but held that if any gods exist, they are too remote to have any interest in human beings. The Stoics believed that happiness comes from a simple acceptance of things as they are, without allowing oneself to yield to the desire for pleasure, and seeking to be free of anger and other disturbing emotions. They emphasised the rational over the emotional, and had a pantheistic view of God as supreme reason.

People with such views were bound to find Paul's message strange. He was, after all, talking about a God who, far from being remote, loved the world and sent his own Son into the world (John 3:16), a Son who lived, died and rose again on the solid ground of this world. Luke tells us that they actually

---

[6] The Good News Bible paraphrases it 'This ignorant show-off', and J. B. Phillips paraphrased the words about bringing strange words as, 'He seems to be trying to proclaim some more gods to us, and outlandish ones at that.'

thought that Paul was proclaiming two gods (maybe a husband and wife team)—Jesus and the resurrection (Jesus and *Anastasis*).

Eventually they brought him to the Areopagus where the Athenian council met, and they said to him, 'May we know what this new teaching is that you are presenting? For you bring some strange things to our ears. We wish to know therefore what these things mean' (Acts 17:19, 20).

Proclaiming Christ

Paul didn't need a second invitation! He may have been marking time in Athens, but here was an opportunity to witness, and he stood in the midst of the Areopagus and spoke to them. He sought a point of contact (as Jesus did with his references to, for example, seeds, salt, yeast and coins) and referred to the altar that he had seen with the inscription, 'To an unknown God.' He went on to say that he wanted to proclaim the truth about what they worshipped as unknown.

He told them that God was no longer unknown. Of course he believed that God had *never* been 'unknown;' he had made himself known partly through creation, partly through planting eternity in the human heart (Eccl. 3:11) and partly through his written word in Scripture. And now (to borrow the language of the Letter to the Hebrews) the God who had spoken 'at many times and in many ways… has spoken to us by his Son' (Heb. 1:1-2)—this Christ Jesus, the man from Nazareth, the Saviour of Calvary, the living Lord.

So, he said to the Athenians, 'What you worship as unknown, this I proclaim to you' (Acts 17:23). He went on to preach the gospel and Luke gives us a snatch of it before Paul was interrupted and prevented from saying everything that he wanted to say.

But, from the 'unknown god' and in response to the many idols of Athens, he preached Christ to them. In terms of what he would later write, it is at the name of Jesus that every knee shall bow (Phil. 2:10), and it is in him that all things hold together (Col. 1:17). Far from Christ being one more deity to be added to the Athenian pantheon, 'There is one God, and there is one mediator between God and men, the man Christ Jesus' (1 Tim. 2:5).

People sometimes imagine that pluralism is a new idea; apparently not. We see it in Athens where allowance was made for everyone's religion, and just in case any god had been missed, there was that catch-all altar, so that any visitors complaining that their god had been missed could be taken to this particular altar (*it's just that we didn't know your god's name*).

Luke also includes the note in verse 21 (perhaps with tongue in cheek) about the Athenians and the foreigners who lived there spending their time in nothing except telling or hearing something new. The people of Athens loved novelty, the excitement of new things, and it perhaps parallels the preference of many today for new ideas and values over truths—even against values that have stood the test of time. It is the preference for political correctness (which 'grips Western culture by the throat'[7]) rather than spiritual and moral correctness, and media-driven celebrity culture rather than the fear of the Lord which is the essence of wisdom.

Many people in our twenty-first century world, especially among the so-called 'chattering classes,' are keen to jettison 'traditional values', without realising that they may be cutting off the branch on which they are sitting. That metaphor was used by the novelist George Orwell when he wrote:

[7] Melanie Phillips, *The World Turned Upside Down* (New York: Encounter Books, 2010), 289.

For two hundred years we had sawed and sawed and sawed at the branch we were sitting on. And in the end, much more suddenly than anyone had foreseen, our efforts were rewarded and down we came. But unfortunately there had been a little mistake: the thing at the bottom was not a bed of roses after all; it was a cesspool full of barbed wire... It appears that amputation of the soul isn't just a simple, surgical job, like having your appendix out. The wound has a tendency to go septic.[8]

In their love for novelty, the Athenians were like the people of Benjamin Warfield's day (Professor of Theology at Princeton Seminary from 1887 to 1921), of whom it has been written, 'The problem of his day was that men would discuss rather than receive truth.'[9] For the Athenians too, a good-going discussion on philosophical or religious subjects was a fine way to while away an afternoon—so long as it didn't make any difference to anything.

Paul's distress

For Paul, however, it was not merely a matter of a theoretical and inconsequential discussion group. When Acts 17:16 says Paul's spirit was provoked within him, the Greek word is the word which gives us the English word 'paroxysm;' his spirit was *paroxysmed* within him. It was originally a medical word, referring to a seizure or fit, and it clearly speaks of a deep-seated disturbance.

For Paul, evangelism was not just a case of sharing his views which people could then take or leave, as if it was a matter of no great consequence. Of course, people *did* have to make up their minds about their response, but it was an agony to him that

---

[8] Quoted (from *Notes on the Way*, 1940) by Vishal Mangalwadi, *The Book that Made your World* (Nashville: Thomas Nelson, 2011), 3.

[9] Fred G. Zaspel, *The Theology of B. B. Warfield* (Nottingham: IVP, 2010), 556.

people were choosing to follow after idols and that they didn't know Jesus. For Paul, the gospel, and people's response to it, is of fundamental importance for their lives in this world and in regard to their eternal destiny.

When I was ordained as a minister, one of the questions put to me was: 'Are not zeal for the glory of God, love to the Lord Jesus Christ, and a desire for the salvation of men, so far as you know your own heart, your great motives and chief inducements to enter into the office of the holy ministry?' To such a question Paul would have answered with a resounding *'Yes'*.

This attitude of heart is a challenge for believers today in this time of widespread scepticism, pluralism and secularism. We are challenged as to whether we merely shrug our shoulders and say 'That's just the way it is', or whether we share anything of Paul's distress about rampant unbelief.

John Stott expressed the challenge in this way: 'Why is it that, in spite of the great needs and opportunities of our day, the church slumbers peacefully on, and that so many Christians are deaf and dumb, deaf to Christ's commission and tongue-tied in testimony? I think the major reason is this: we do not speak as Paul spoke because we do not feel as Paul felt.'[10]

In parallel to what was said above about the positive blessings known by the Athenians:

- Many people today have far more in the way of possessions and luxuries than previous generations had—but what if they don't have Christ in their hearts?

- They may be able to afford holidays—even visits to Athens—but what if they don't have Christ in their hearts?

[10] John Stott, *The Message of Acts* (Leicester: IVP, 1990), 290.

- We may be better educated today than ever, but what if that just makes us cleverer fools?

- We have wonderful healthcare and increasing longevity, but what if we are unprepared for what comes after our life in this world, however long or short it may be?

- People may have a very comfortable lifestyle and seem to live contented lives, but what good is it to gain the whole world if you lose your soul? (Mark 8:36).

For Paul there was an urgency (1 Cor. 9:16) about proclaiming the gospel of forgiveness, life, peace and eternal salvation in Christ. We know, especially from his letter to the Romans, that Paul emphasised the effects of the *death* of Christ, but in Athens it was the proclamation of the *resurrection* that provoked a response (though obviously he could not have referred to Jesus' resurrection without having first spoken of the cross); his whole message centred in Jesus who both died and rose again.

His hearers came to realise that he wasn't only speaking about a great hero who was dead and gone; he wasn't giving good advice about a great example or a teacher whom everyone should follow. He was talking about a Saviour who died on the cross but who rose again from the dead; he was talking about a living Christ. Jesus is not someone who was alive and is now dead but someone who was dead and is now alive.

And it was that reference to the resurrection that caused everything to go up in the air. The one-time enemy of Christ saw varying responses to his testimony to Christ. Some people mocked him and his message. One can almost hear them: 'This is nonsense; we all know that when people die, they rot in the ground—end of story. How can you expect us intelligent first century people to believe that Jesus rose from the dead—we're not in the dark ages, you know!'

Others responded to Paul's message by playing for time. They said, 'We will hear you again about this' (Acts 17:32). That may have been genuine; maybe they did want time to reflect, and it is true that people should not be bull-dozed into quick and hasty decisions. Yet it is also true that decisions that are delayed become more and more difficult. We all know that in every-day affairs (even simple things like writing a letter or email, or going on a diet), and it is true in the most important things of all—decisions delayed become more and more unlikely ever to be made.

C. S. Lewis wrote about the need to stop procrastinating and come to Christ in repentance and faith. In a chapter headed 'The Practical Conclusion', he was answering people who ask why God has not 'landed in force in this enemy-occupied world':

> But I wonder whether people who ask God to interfere openly and directly in our world quite realise what it will be like when He does. When this happens, it is the end of the world... It will be too late then to choose your side. There is no use saying you choose to lie down when it has become impossible to stand up. That will not be the time for choosing: it will be the time when we discover which side we really have chosen, whether we realised it before or not. Now, today, this moment, is our chance to choose the right side. God is holding back to give us that chance. It will not last for ever.[11]

Best of all is to deliberately make that choice, as we are told Dionysius and Damaris did, along with others who believed and committed themselves to Christ. Then, like Paul, we can say, 'I know whom I have believed, and I am convinced that he is

---

[11] C. S. Lewis, *Mere Christianity* (London: Collins, 1952), 63.

able to guard until that Day what has been entrusted to me'—this message about 'the appearing of our Saviour Jesus Christ, who abolished death and brought life and immortality to light through the gospel' (2 Tim. 1:10-12).

Paul's strategy

It is also true that Paul didn't plough straight in. As he responded to the invitation to explain his new teaching, he started with creation, referring in verse 24 to 'The God who made the world and everything in it' Acts 17:24), and then he took up the theme of providence in verses 26-28 about how it is in him that we live and move and have our being. After laying that groundwork, he then came to revelation—the truth that God has made himself known. Then he spoke of Jesus and emphasised the urgency of the fact that God has 'fixed a day on which he will judge the world in righteousness by a man whom he has appointed; and of this he has given assurance to all by raising him from the dead' (Acts 17:31).

Acts 17 tells us not only of Paul's message but also of his methods. It is a picture of a great Christian witness and evangelist in action. We are told that he 'reasoned' with people (Acts 17:17). People need to know that Christianity is not just a set of mythical stories and that it does not lack intellectual credibility. No-one can be argued into the kingdom of God, and while we are dependent upon the work of the Holy Spirit in other people's hearts, it is also important that the gospel should be made known in a reasoned way. As Peter said, we should be ready to give a reason for the hope we have, doing so with respect (1 Pet. 3:15).

We also see Paul taking opportunities where they presented themselves, whether in the synagogue with the Jews and god-fearers there, or in the market-place (the *agora*) with whoever happened to be there—not only in church, so to speak, but out in the midst of the everyday world of daily life.

The real truth

We are concerned in this book with *the gospel according to Christ's enemies* and when they heard Paul speaking about Jesus and the Resurrection (Acts 17:18) and remarked that he was bringing new teaching to them, they spoke the truth, albeit unintentionally. He *was* indeed bringing a new message—a message about new birth (John 3:3), a message about 'a new and living way' (Heb. 10:20) to peace with God.

As Paul wrote to the Corinthians, it is 'of first importance' that 'Christ died for our sins in accordance with the Scriptures, that he was buried, that he was raised on the third day in accordance with the Scriptures, and that he appeared' to many people (1 Cor. 15:3-5). If he had not died and risen again, Paul went on to argue in that passage, there would be no faith ('your faith would be in vain'), there would be no forgiveness ('still in your sins') and there would be no future ('those who have fallen asleep in Christ have perished'). But in fact Christ was raised from the dead and Paul was truly a preacher of Jesus and *Anastasis*, Jesus and the resurrection.

The Oxford scientist and mathematician John Lennox has emphasised the crucial importance of the resurrection;

> From the very start, the leaders of the Christian community staked the whole validity of the gospel message upon it… disprove the resurrection, and the whole of Christianity would disappear in a puff of smoke. Unlike most other religions and worldviews which are based on ideas or theories, Christianity claims to be falsifiable, based on this single historical claim. Disprove the resurrection of Jesus, and Christianity is dead.'[12]

[12] *Can Science Explain Everything* (New Malden: The Good Book Company, 2019), 89-90.

In Athens Paul proclaimed Jesus and the resurrection, and the end of the chapter tells us that some who may have started off as enemies when they first heard Paul, became believers. Others remained enemies as they mocked Paul and his message, while others tried to sit on the fence—'We will hear you again about this' (Acts 17:32-34).

Paul was not a mere *spermologos*, someone picking up bits and pieces here and there and combining them into a mishmash religion. His message came to him from God.

He himself would once have laughed at the idea that he might become a follower of Christ. He had been an fierce enemy of Christianity, and later he would sometimes recall the days when he was an enemy of Christ. On several occasions he referred to it:

- Acts 22:4-5—'I persecuted this Way to the death, binding and delivering to prison both men and women.'

- Acts 26:10-11—'I not only locked up many of the saints in prison after receiving authority from the chief priests, but when they were put to death I cast my vote against them. And I punished them often in all the synagogues and tried to make them blaspheme, and in raging fury against them I persecuted them even to foreign cities.'

- 1 Corinthians 15:9—'I am the least of the apostles, unworthy to be called an apostle, because I persecuted the church of God.'

- Galatians 1:13—'You have heard of my former life in Judaism, how I persecuted the church of God violently and tried to destroy it.'

- Philippians 3:6—'… as to zeal (I was) a persecutor of the church.'

- 1 Timothy 1:13—'Formerly I was a blasphemer, persecutor, and insolent opponent.'

It seems as if he could never forget that he himself had once been such an enemy of Christianity and of Christ; and if he himself would once have laughed at the idea that he might become a servant of that gospel, we may be encouraged that some who scoff may be won round by the grace of God.

In the last passage quoted above, Paul went on,

> I received mercy because I had acted ignorantly in unbelief, and the grace of our Lord overflowed for me with the faith and love that are in Christ Jesus. The saying is trustworthy and deserving of full acceptance, that Christ Jesus came into the world to save sinners, of whom I am the foremost. But I received mercy for this reason, that in me, as the foremost, Jesus Christ might display his perfect patience as an example to those who were to believe in him for eternal life' (1 Tim. 1:13-16).

Such is the gospel according to 'this babbler', a man who was once an enemy of Christ, but who became a follower and servant of that same Christ. 'I have been crucified with Christ,' he wrote. 'It is no longer I who live, but Christ who lives in me. And the life I now live in the flesh I live by faith in the Son of God, who loved me and gave himself for me' (Gal. 2:20).

11

Christ's Enemies
According to the Gospel

We have been considering the gospel according to Christ's enemies, but what if we were to turn the phrase round and ask about *Christ's enemies according to the gospel* (or the Bible)? That will be the subject of this chapter, and then in the final chapter I will reflect upon *the gospel according to Christ*.

If all that the Bible says about Christ is right, then the question, 'What about Christ's enemies according to the gospel?' is a very important one. As has often been said, our opinions about God are far less important than God's opinion about us!

In one sense, the Bible describes us *all* as God's enemies. Paul wrote, 'All have sinned and fall short of the glory of God' (Rom. 3:23) and 'we were enemies' (Rom. 5:10). And the gospel is all about being changed from enemies into friends, from unconcerned sinners to sinners who are being saved by grace.

Writing to Christian converts, Paul would bid them 'remember that you were at that time separated from Christ… having no hope and without God in the world' (Eph. 2:12), and he referred to non-Christians as 'darkened in their understanding, alienated from the life of God because of the ignorance that is in them, due to their hardness of heart' (Eph. 4:18).

It is not a flattering description of unredeemed human beings, but it is the dark background against which the gospel of grace shines all the more brightly.

Christ's attitude to his enemies

In the introduction we set the attitude of Christ's enemies to him in the context of *his* attitude toward his enemies. He spoke about loving one's enemies (Matt. 5:44) and he also demonstrated it, even in the extremities of death by crucifixion as he prayed, 'Father, forgive them, for they know not what they do' (Luke 23:34).

The Bible speaks about his patience. Peter wrote about the coming 'Day of the Lord' and, in response to people who imply that it will never come, he wrote, 'The Lord is not slow to fulfil his promise as some count slowness, but is patient towards you, not wishing that any should perish, but that all should reach repentance' (2 Pet. 3:9).

However, he immediately went on, 'But the day of the Lord will come,' and although Paul spoke of the patience of the Lord as our salvation (2 Pet. 3:15) he emphasised that that patience should not lead people into complacency. The solemn truth about Christ's enemies, according to the Bible, is that if they continue in a state of alienation, what lies ahead is judgement and condemnation.

Coming judgement

The Bible's teaching about judgement and hell is one of its least popular aspects, but its reality is unaffected by its popularity or unpopularity. Certain conditions and events have consequences, whether we like it or not.

We know this in ordinary matters. We warn children not to play with fire because we know that fire burns and injures people. The reason why there are such things as speed limits and zero tolerance of driving under the influence of alcohol is that we know the tragic consequences that can be caused by such irresponsible actions.

And in even more important issues, the Bible warns about the terrible consequences of remaining in a state of sinful alienation from our Maker. The terrible truth about Christ's enemies according to the Bible is that if people persist in their rejection of the gospel, then there can only be 'a fearful expectation of judgement, and a fury of fire that will consume the adversaries' (Heb. 10:27).

Many people mock, hate, and reject such teaching, but just as we would not want to be treated by a physician who says he doesn't believe in cancer, so we need to pay attention to reality rather than what we might wish to be the case. C. S. Lewis wrote on this topic, saying:

> In the long run the answer to all those who object to the doctrine of hell, is itself a question: 'What are you asking God to do?' To wipe out their past sins and, at all costs, to give them a fresh start, smoothing every difficulty and offering every miraculous help? But He has done so, on Calvary. To forgive them? They will not be forgiven. To leave them alone? Alas, I am afraid that is what He does.[1]

He also wrote, 'Christianity now has to preach the diagnosis—in itself very bad news—before it can win a hearing for the cure… A recovery of the old sense of sin is essential to Christianity.[2] So long as people deny the existence of their disease or illness, little can be done about it, and if people deny the reality of their sin and rebellion, they deny themselves the wonderful news of the remedy.

---

[1] *The Problem of Pain* (London: Geoffrey Bles, 1940), 116.
[2] *Ibid.*, 43-5.

Sometimes it has been claimed or implied that 'religious people' have taken delight in the thought of judgement and hell. If that has been true, it has been a denial of what we read in the Scriptures. Think, for example, of Jeremiah, sometimes known as the weeping prophet, who wrote, in connection with the calamity (defeat and exile) coming upon his people because of their rebellion, 'Oh, that my head were waters and my eyes a fountain of tears, that I might weep day and night for the slain of my people' (Jer. 9:1).

The well-known words of Jesus, 'Blessed are those who mourn' (Matt. 5:4) are often applied to the experience of grief and bereavement, but they also describe the blessedness of those who share the grief in the heart of God over human rebellion against all that makes for their true well-being, peace and eternal bliss.

This is the God who spoke through the prophet Ezekiel: 'As I live, I have no pleasure in the death of the wicked, but that the wicked turn from his way and live; turn back, turn back from your evil ways, for why will you die, O house of Israel?' (Ezek. 33:11).

When Jeremiah thought about the plight of his people, he wrote, 'My anguish, my anguish! I writhe in pain,' (Jer. 4:19), and the Bible encourages such an attitude of concern in regard to the ways in which human beings still rebel against their Maker and turn away from godliness.

Rather than enjoying the thought of hell and revelling in the preaching of it, the godly way is to grieve over the prospect of people being cut off from God, which is what hell means.

Christ's enemy

This book is about unintended expressions of gospel truth from people who opposed and hated Jesus. Behind it all, the ultimate enemy of God and man is the devil. Very near the beginning of the Bible we read what has been called the *protoevangelium*, the first announcement of the gospel. God's word to the devil was, 'I will put enmity between you and the woman, and between your offspring and her offspring; he shall bruise your head, and you shall bruise his heel' (Gen. 3:15).

Centuries later it happened. The incarnate Son was 'bruised' at Calvary. But it was through his act of self-sacrifice and atonement that he overcame the devil. He took on flesh 'that through death he might destroy the one who has the power of death, that is, the devil, and deliver all those who through fear of death were subject to lifelong slavery' (Heb. 2:14, 15). 'The reason the Son of God appeared was to destroy the works of the devil' (1 John 3:8).

At the very beginning of Jesus' incarnate life, the devil sought to eliminate him. The apostle John expressed it with rich symbolism in the book of Revelation. He referred to a great sign that appeared in heaven—

> And behold, a great red dragon… stood before the woman who was about to give birth, so that when she bore the child he might devour it. She gave birth to a male child, one who is to rule all the nation with a rod of iron, but her child was caught up to God and to his throne (Rev. 12:1-6).

So it was as Satan worked through Herod, seeking to get rid of the infant Jesus as soon as he was born (Matt. 2), but the angel of the Lord led Joseph to take the child and his mother to Egypt and only return after Herod had died.

Then at the outset of Jesus' public ministry, the devil sought to turn him aside from his purpose in coming. Matthew, Mark and Luke tell of the temptation of Christ in the wilderness.

The tempter came and said to him, 'If you are the Son of God, command these stones to become loaves of bread.'… Then the devil took him to the holy city and set him on the pinnacle of the temple and said to him, 'If you are the Son of God, throw yourself down, for it is written, "He will command his angels concerning you", and "On their hands they will bear you up, lest you strike your foot against a stone."'… Again, the devil took him to a very high mountain and showed him all the kingdoms of the world and their glory. And he said to him, 'All these I will give you, if you will fall down and worship me' (Matt. 4:1-11).

In these ways the devil tempted him to turn aside from the task that he had come to accomplish, but each time Jesus resisted the temptation, quoting the words of Scripture:

'It is written, "Man shall not live by bread alone, but by every word that comes from the mouth of God."'

'You shall not put the Lord your God to the test.'

'Be gone, Satan! For it is written, "You shall worship the Lord your God and him only shall you serve."'

Luke's gospel tells us that the devil then 'departed from him until an opportune time' (Luke 4:13), indicating that this was not the only occasion when Jesus was tempted to turn to another way. Satan would speak through the words of the apostle Peter (Matt. 16:23), the actions of Judas (Luke 22:34), and the machinations of the religious leaders of the Jews (Matt. 27:1).

But through it all, Jesus refused to turn aside from his purpose. 'Though he was in the form of God, he did not count equality with God a thing to be grasped, but emptied himself, by taking the form of a servant… He humbled himself by becoming obedient to the point of death, even death on a cross' (Phil. 2:7-8). Supremely at Calvary, he resisted, overcame, and destroyed the works of the devil.

It is obvious that the devil is still active in the world but the truth about this terrible enemy of Christ is that his power has been overcome and the time will come when that residual power will be finally crushed.

Then death itself will be finally defeated. Paul writes of Christ's resurrection as the guarantee of this:

> Christ has been raised from the dead, the firstfruits of those who have fallen asleep. For as by a man came death, by a man has come the resurrection of the dead. For as in Adam all die, so also in Christ shall all be made alive. But each in his own order: Christ the firstfruits, then at his coming those who belong to Christ. Then comes the end, when he delivers the kingdom to God the Father after destroying every rule and every authority and power. For he must reign until he has put all his enemies under his feet. The last enemy to be destroyed is death. (1 Cor. 15:20-26)

The opening of the books

The book of Revelation tells of John's vision:

> Then I saw the dead, great and small, standing before the throne, and books were opened. Then another book was opened, which is the book of life. And the dead were judged by what was written in the books, according to what they had done... And if anyone's name was not found written in the book of life, he was thrown into the lake of fire (Rev. 20:12-15).

Revelation begins with the assertion that God gave its message to John 'to show to his servant the things that must soon take place' (Rev. 1:1). It is a revelation, an apocalypse—the word signifies something that *was* hidden but is hidden no longer. Sadly, the book has sometimes been treated as if it had been intended to *conceal* the truth rather than reveal it, but it was written for a very practical purpose. Much of its message is expressed in colourful and highly symbolic terms, but its message is an essentially practical one. As Revelation 14:12 says (in the NIV translation), 'This calls for patient endurance on the part of the saints who obey God's commandments and remain faithful to Jesus.'

A well-known hymn expresses this practical intent well when it says:

> And when the strife is fierce, the warfare long,
> Steals on the ear the distant triumph song,
> And hearts are brave again and arms are strong.
> Hallelujah.[3]

As we pay heed to the things revealed in Revelation—and in the Bible as a whole—that song of victory 'steals on the ear,' and it is a song of triumph. The enemies of God and of Christ will one day have to bow the knee and acknowledge that Jesus Christ is Lord (Phil 2:10. 11), whether that acknowledgment is one of love and worship, or one of fear and trembling. His victory is assured.

When the early church came to write the story of the martyrdom of the elderly bishop Polycarp of Smyrna who was burned alive in the arena, they were careful to record the exact date. This how it was put: 'Polycarp was martyred, Statius Quadratus being proconsul of Asia and Jesus Christ being King for ever.'[4] Who has heard of Statius Quadratus now? Yet the name of Polycarp is remembered even after all these centuries because of his faithfulness to Christ—and of course Jesus' name will be known for ever.

My wife once did some secretarial work for a theologian who had been President of Princeton Theological Seminary in the USA, and who in 1952 wrote a *Letter to Presbyterians*. It was

---

[3] Hymn, 'For All the Saints' by William Walsham How (1823–97).
[4] *Ante-Nicene Fathers*, Vol. I, Chapter XXI in: http://www.sacred-texts.com/chr/ecf/001/0010119.htm (accessed 16 November 2018).

written against the background of so-called McCarthyism, which was the tendency to see communist threats everywhere. What he wrote reads rather remarkably in light of events that transpired later in the twentieth century. It begins, 'Just because God rules in the affairs of men, communism as a solution of the human problem is foredoomed to failure. No political order can prevail which deliberately leaves God out of account.'

His words proved to be remarkably prophetic, in light of what happened about forty years later: 'The communistic order will eventually be shattered upon the bedrock of human nature, that is, upon the basic sins and the abysmal needs, of man and society. For that reason communism has an approaching rendezvous with God and the moral order.'[5]

That was, he wrote, God's message for God-denying and God-defying communism, but truly it is God's message for every system (including capitalism if it denies and defies God)—but not referring only to issues of economic theory. These words about 'an approaching rendezvous with God' give us the Bible's message for everyone. We must all appear before the judgement-seat of Christ (2 Cor. 5:10).

This is an unwelcome thought for many people, people like the former British Poet Laureate who answered the question, 'What do you think death is?' with, 'Nothing. The only thing that keeps me awake sweating at night is the idea that there might be something. I just want to go out like a light.'[6] That may be the wish, the hope even, of many people, but according to Jesus Christ and the Bible, it is a vain hope.

The truth is: 'It is appointed for man to die once, and after that comes judgement' (Heb. 9:27). And for those who choose to

---

[5] Princeton Theological Seminary *Alumni News*, Volume 23, No.3, Spring 1983.

[6] Andrew Motion in response to Joan Bakewell: *Belief* (London: Duckworth, 2005), 227.

remain enemies of Christ there can only be what the Bible itself bluntly calls 'a fearful expectation of judgement, and a fury of fire that will consume the adversaries' (Heb. 10:27).

It is an extremely unwelcome aspect of the Bible's teaching for many. Many people want what Richard Niebuhr characterised as 'a God without wrath bringing people without sin into a kingdom without judgment through the ministrations of a Christ without a cross.'[7] But our concern ought to be with reality rather than with our own preferences. The person who tells you that you are in danger from a speeding vehicle or a falling rock may disturb your peace of mind, but that person is truly the friend who cares about your welfare.

When Elijah confronted king Ahab with the wickedness of his actions in stealing a vineyard which properly belonged to Naboth, Ahab spat out, 'Have you found me, O my enemy?' (1 Kings 21:20). Earlier he had called Elijah a troubler of Israel (1 Kings 18:17)—which was rich, as we say, coming from him! The truth is that Ahab, with his rebellion against God and rejection of his ways, was the real troubler of the land, and far from regarding Elijah as his enemy, he should have welcomed him as the best friend he could have, one who would encourage him to repent and honour the Lord and his ways.

The Bible, far from being our enemy by telling us unwelcome things, is truly God's message of love that bids us turn from our sin and selfishness and to come to him in repentance and trust. And its teaching about what happens to the enemies of Christ is not given as an idle threat, as if it were crying wolf when there is no wolf. No-one had more to say about judgement and hell than Jesus, and his teaching is given in love. He did not come to

---

[7] Richard Niebuhr, *The Kingdom of God in America* (Middletown, CT: Wesleyan University Press, 1988), 193.

condemn the world but in order that the world might be saved (John 3:17), but what a fearful thing it is to fall into the hands of the living God. (Heb 10:31).

God calls us to repent and accept the great salvation which is the gift of his grace to all who will receive it. This is the gospel of Christ, which will be the subject of our last chapter.

The Gospel According to Christ

The Bible says that we all are—or were—God's enemies. We are fallen human beings who inherited a sinful nature and the gospel is all about what God has done on his own initiative to overcome that hostility. The good news for those who put their trust in Christ as their Saviour is—'You who once were alienated and hostile in mind, doing evil deeds, he has now reconciled in his body of flesh by his death in order to present you holy and blameless and above reproach before him' (Col. 1:21-22). Paul also wrote, 'If while we were enemies we were reconciled to God by the death of his Son, much more, now that we are reconciled, shall we be saved by his life' (Rom. 5:10). The verse before that says, 'God shows his love for us in that while we were still sinners, Christ died for us.'

There is no room for boasting of any kind (Eph. 2:9). If we are Christians at all, it is only through the grace of God who has had mercy on those who were, by nature, his enemies.

This is the point emphasised by one of my teachers at divinity college:

> It is only when we actually know Christ, know him as our personal Saviour and Lord, that we know that we have not

chosen him but that he has chosen us; that it is not in our capacity to give ourselves the power to know him; that it is not in virtue of our own power or our own capacity that he gives us to know him, but in virtue of his power to reveal himself to us and to enable us to know him; that is, faith itself is the gift of God. Or let me put it another way: when we know God in Christ, we do not congratulate ourselves on our own powers of intuition or discovery and pat ourselves on the back because we have been able to see that there is more in Jesus than meets the eye, that God is there himself. No, we do the exact opposite: we acknowledge that in knowing God in Christ, we do so not by our own power, but by the power of God.[1]

One of the consequences of being his is that we grieve over those who remain enemies of Christ. That was the spirit in which Paul wrote, for example in Philippians 3:18 'Many, of whom I have often told you and now tell you even with tears, walk as enemies of the cross of Christ.'

This is the tragic truth. It is tragic that many people are not only God's enemies unawares, but that many deliberately set themselves against the message of Christ.

Contemporary secularisation

Evidence of secularisation is not lacking for anyone with eyes that are open to what is happening. Secularism threatens to engulf Western society, including even parts of the professing church. Whereas unbelievers would once have kept their heads down out of deference to Christians and Christianity, there is now an attitude of open and increasingly aggressive opposition. This is promulgated by well-known and high-profile atheists, but anti-Christian views are also pushed repeatedly and blatantly

[1] T. F. Torrance, *Incarnation* (Milton Keynes: Paternoster, 2008), 2.

by the pervasive entertainment industry, probably with more effect than that of the more 'intellectual' enemies of the gospel.

The veteran British broadcaster John Humphrys, who professes to be neither a believer nor an atheist but an agnostic, has poked fun at today's militant atheists by summing up their attitude in seven statements:

1. Believers are mostly naïve or stupid. Or, at least, they're not as clever as atheists.
2. The few clever ones are pathetic because they need a crutch to get them through life.
3. They are also pathetic because they can't accept the finality of death.
4. They have been brainwashed into believing. There is no such thing as a 'Christian child,' for instance—just a child whose parents have had her baptised.
5. They have been bullied into believing.
6. If we don't wipe out religious belief by next Thursday week, civilisation as we know it is doomed.
7. Trust me: I'm an atheist.[2]

He goes on to comment on each of these points but, without going into them again, his tongue-in-cheek summary does serve to highlight some of the fatuous nonsense that is spread about today. Yet, many people buy into the assumption that religion has had its day.

But it is no laughing matter and one can only fear for the future of a society that is becoming increasingly illiberal in its attitudes, and in which attempts are made to even close off one occupation or career after another to people who take a biblical view on issues of life and morality.

[2] John Humphrys, *In God We Doubt* (London: Hodder & Stoughton, 2007), 333f.

All of this is true, but perhaps the very fact that today's secularising atheists are so vociferous and belligerent may be, in a way, a good sign. Whether or not they still unintentionally say things that are intended as attacks but turn out to be true, the attacks at least show a realisation that there is something worth attacking.

The apostle Peter encouraged his readers to not be surprised when attacks and opposition came upon the early church—'as though something strange were happening to you... Let none of you suffer as a murderer or a thief or an evildoer or as a meddler. Yet if anyone suffers as a Christian, let him not be ashamed, but let him glorify God in that name' (1 Pet. 4:12-16).

Peter's message for a beleaguered church was and is: when opposition comes—don't be surprised, don't be depressed, don't be ashamed and don't be paralysed. After all, Peter had heard Jesus himself saying to his disciples, 'Woe to you, when all people speak well of you' (Luke 6:26), and the apostle Paul wrote, 'All who desire to live a godly life in Christ Jesus will be persecuted' (2 Tim. 3:12).

Obviously no one should seek persecution or court unpopularity—Christians are meant to live lives that 'adorn the doctrine of God our Saviour' (Titus 2:10; the NIV translates it, '...so that in every way they will make the teaching about God our Saviour attractive')—but these various verses suggest that the absence of any opposition or pressure should be more alarming than their presence. Far better a situation in which Christianity is thought to be worth attacking than one where it is ignored and thought to be not worth opposing.

One of the seven churches addressed in Revelation 2 and 3 is the church of Sardis, which was said to have the name of being alive but was dead (Rev. 3:1). One commentary has described it in these terms:

> This is a church which everyone speaks well of, the perfect model of inoffensive Christianity, unable to distinguish between the peace of well-being and the peace of death… Content with mediocrity, lacking both the enthusiasm to entertain a heresy and the depth of conviction which provokes intolerance, it was too innocuous to be worth persecuting.[3]

How terrible an indictment would that be—to be a church that isn't worth persecuting.

During George Whitefield's time in eighteenth-century Britain, there were attacks on Christianity and Christians. On one occasion, his friend Benjamin Franklin had been subjected to strong criticism in various newspapers. Franklin's relatives were upset for him, but Franklin advised them not to be too upset as he could recall something which Mr Whitefield had said to him in a similar situation: 'When I am on the Road, and see Boys in a Field at a Distance, pelting a tree, though I am too far off to know what Tree it is, I conclude it has FRUIT on it.'[4]

Perhaps the very fact that increasingly strident attacks are made on Christianity gives evidence that the Christian tree is bearing fruit, that there is something to attack.

As a matter of fact, the church has frequently grown stronger and more vibrant in times of persecution than in times of peace and quiet. So Richard Bewes could write:

> We Christians today are astonished, not so much at the ever-continuing advance in the 2.3 billion-strong family of Jesus Christ worldwide, but rather at the amazing failure of

[3] G. B. Caird, *The Revelation of St. John the Divine* (New York: Harper & Row, 1966), 48.

[4] A. Dallimore, *George Whitefield* (Edinburgh: Banner of Truth, 1980), 451.

our critics to learn from history. Naturally we weep when a Janani Luwum (Uganda), of a Mehdi Dibaj (Iran) is martyred. Such martyrs are numbered by the thousand today, as they were 20 centuries ago. But the sweep of civilisation indicates that the greater the persecution on the church from its outside persecutors, the stronger tends to be its growth.[5]

Two illustrations

I conclude with two interesting illustrations of the impact of Christianity on Christ's enemies. One is an article by the journalist Matthew Parris under the intriguing heading, 'As an atheist, I truly believe Africa needs God.' As an atheist he might be expected to be opposed to Christianity, but he had returned after forty-five years to Malawi (Nyasaland when he was a boy) to visit a Pump Aid project, and he wrote about it:

> It inspired me, renewing my flagging faith in development charities. But travelling in Malawi refreshed another belief, too, one I've been trying to banish all my life, but an observation I've been unable to avoid since my African childhood. It confounds my ideological beliefs, stubbornly refuses to fit my world view, and has embarrassed my growing belief that there is no God. Now a confirmed atheist, I've become convinced of the enormous contribution that Christian evangelism makes in Africa, sharply distinct from the work of secular NGOs, government projects and international aid efforts. These alone will not do. Education and training alone will not do. In Africa Christianity changes people's hearts. It brings a spiritual transformation. The rebirth is real. The change is good.[6]

He went on to say that he used to applaud the practical work of mission churches in Africa and then add, 'It's a pity that salvation

[5] Article in *Evangelicals Now*, December 2012.
[6] The *Times*, 27 December 2008.

is part of the package. I would allow that if faith was needed to motivate missionaries to help, then, fine but what counted was the help, not the faith. But this doesn't fit the facts.'

And in his concluding sentences, he wrote:

> Those who want Africa to walk tall amid 21st century global competition must not kid themselves that providing the material means or even the knowledge that accompanies what we call development will make them change. A whole belief system must first be supplanted. And I'm afraid it has to be supplanted by another. Removing Christian evangelism from the African equation may leave the continent at the mercy of a malign fusion of Nike, the witch doctor, the mobile phone and the machete.

It is a fascinating article, and what was that title again? 'As an atheist, I truly believe Africa needs God.' So does every other part of the world, and it is fascinating that even critics and enemies of the gospel should be forced into such an admission.

The other interesting illustration of the impact of Christianity on the enemies of Christ is found in the development of churches for the godless (although one adherent has described that term as an oxymoron). If imitation is the sincerest form of flattery, then the church should be highly flattered!

Not all leaders or members of the new movement would say they are actual enemies of Christianity, but their development does point to the need for 'something', even when the people are opposed to Christianity.

One blogger has written of his departure from the Christian church:

> I like his [God's] family, on the whole. Some of them are a bit weird, but mostly we get along. In fact, that's one thing I do miss since we split: those family gatherings; the singing; the regular opportunity to reflect on my life and on how it might

be lived better, for myself and for others. I couldn't keep going back to church to join them though; I wouldn't have enjoyed it and they wouldn't have wanted an 'ex' hanging around the place either.

'Fortunately, I have found a church-equivalent: a community of like-minded people who gather, on a Sunday as it happens, to be inspired, to think about life, to help one another, and to sing their hearts out! It's called the Sunday Assembly. It's a godless congregation that seeks to help people to live their lives to their full potential. Their motto is, 'Live Better, Help Often, Wonder More.' The first time I attended an Assembly meeting I walked in to hear a brass band playing loud enough to lift the roof off and then I sat down to listen to a talk on the universe by a physicist from CERN. I thought I'd died and gone to heaven!

'During the 'services' (there's no better word) there is always some time for reflection and there's always an inspiring talk which challenges and engages. Oh, and the singing... did I mention the singing? I love it![7]

Perhaps it's a passing fad that will soon die a natural death. It is certainly unlikely to outlive the church's record of longevity. A 2019 article in the American magazine, *The Atlantic*, suggested that the trend may not have much staying power. It referred to someone who moved to New York City nine years previously, leaving behind her church, her God and her old city (Los Angeles). There she found a secular assembly, 'founded by faithless

[7]   http://www.huffingtonpost.co.uk/paul-beaumont/losing-faith_b_5889466. html (accessed 16 March 2018). Interestingly, Billy Graham wrote about this trend more than half a century ago: 'Julian Huxley said that if humanism is to acquire a wider appeal, it must become a religion, while another humanist, L. F. J. Ross, suggests that "a simple humanist bible and humanist hymns must be adopted, a ten commandments for humanists could be added, as could humanist confessional practices for groups or individuals…The use of hypnotic techniques, music and other devices during humanist services would give the audience their deep spiritual experience, and they would emerge refreshed and inspired with their humanist faith.' *World Aflame* (New York: Doubleday, 1965), 53.

158

seekers hoping to carry on certain aspects of religious life: the community, the moral deliberation and the rich sense of wonder.' For a while this secular Sunday Assembly filled the spiritual void but after a couple of years 'things began to fall apart' and the article tells of the closing down of the chapter in early 2016, three years after its opening. The decline of the movement as a whole has been marked, with the number of chapters falling from 70 to 40 within three years and attendances from about 5,000 in 2016 to about 3,500 in 2018. The article quotes some leaders as saying that they tried to make the meetings so interesting, entertaining and powerful that people would keep showing up, but it turns out to be not so easy![8]

The prolific writer Sabine Baring-Gould wrote about the enduring nature of the church in his hymn:

> Crowns and thrones may perish,
>   Kingdoms rise and wane,
> But the Church of Jesus
>   Constant will remain.

It goes on:

> Gates of hell can never
>   'Gainst that Church prevail

Why? Not because it is a well-organised human force or because it has managed to exert some kind of worldly authority; it is because 'We have Christ's own promise and that cannot fail.'[9]

Such words might seem bombastic and even belligerent, but the sentiment is not a boast about the superior staying-power of the church as a human institution. It is Jesus himself who says that the gates of hell shall not prevail against the church (Matt.

---

[8] www.theatlantic.com/ideas/archive/2019/07/secular-churches-rethink-their-sales-pitch/594109 (accessed 22 July 2019).

[9] Hymn, 'Onward, Christian Soldiers' by Sabine Baring-Gould (1834–1924).

16:18), and 'I am alive for evermore, and I have the keys of Death and Hades' (Rev. 1:18). In the latter verse it is the second 'I' that should be emphasised. It is the victorious Christ who has the power and authority—not the seemingly-invincible Caesars of that day, or any of the other powers that have risen and waned through the centuries.

As far as churches for the godless are concerned, they are unlikely to last for decades to come; for one thing, the idea of a non-belief being your central belief is not easy to fathom or to sustain. But their unabashed aping of church life points to something deep and radical about our human needs. Perhaps they are simply after a sense of community—but is there more to it than that? Ecclesiastes 3:11 says that God has 'put eternity into man's heart,' which means that without him life will always be lacking the vital ingredient for fulness of life here and for assurance of eternal life in the age to come.

And that brings us back to the gospel. The Bible says, 'If you confess with your mouth that Jesus is Lord and believe in your heart that God raised him from the dead, you will be saved' (Rom. 10:9). This is the Lord described by Paul as 'The Son of God who loved me and gave himself for me' (Gal. 2:20).

Accused of many things

Apart from the comments from the enemies of Christianity which we have considered in earlier pages, the Bible tells of many other words that were spoken against Christ. Mark 15:3 tells us, 'The chief priests accused him of many things.' That was in the context of the events that led to the crucifixion, but it was true all through the three-year period of his public ministry that people 'accused him of many things.' For example, they called him a blasphemer (Matt. 9:3) and a Sabbath-breaker (Matt. 12:2). They said he was in league with the devil (Matt. 12:24) and they attacked him when his disciples were seen eating without going through their handwashing rituals (Matt. 15:2).

And there are some other places in the gospels where we find unintended testimony to gospel truth from Christ's enemies. One interesting comment is found in the aftermath of the raising of Lazarus. John 11 tells of that amazing miracle and we learn that Jesus' Jewish enemies were greatly troubled by it. Always on the lookout for things they could use against him, they 'made plans to put Lazarus to death, because on account of him many of the Jews were going away and believing in Jesus' (John 12:10, 11). *Shock, horror! This has gone too far—we have to stop him.* Yet they faced the uncomfortable fact that Lazarus could be seen walking the lanes of the village of Bethany!

That was followed by the public spectacle of Jesus' so-called triumphal entry into Jerusalem, when crowds turned out to welcome him, and John tells us, 'The Pharisees said to one another, "You see that you are gaining nothing. Look, the world has gone after him"' (John 12:19). How right they were! And ever since then, the message of the gospel has been proclaimed all over the world and millions of people have 'gone after him.'

We also find these same enemies giving unintended testimony to the truth about Jesus in Matthew 22:16: 'They sent their disciples to him, along with the Herodians, saying, "Teacher, we know that you are true and teach the way of God truthfully, and you do not care about anyone's opinion, for you are not swayed by appearances."' They didn't intend to compliment Jesus but they were right—Jesus was not like the chameleon that changes colour according to its surroundings.

They also tried to land him in hot water with their question about whether people should pay taxes to Rome (the occupying power). If he said *No*, they would be able to report his words to the Roman overlords, and if he said *Yes* that would antagonise the Jews who hated the fact that they were under Roman domination. This attempt failed, and *they* were the ones left with egg on their faces as Jesus gave his famous answer, 'Render to Caesar the things that are Caesar's, *and* to God the things that are God's' (Matt. 22:21, probably with the emphasis on the second half of the saying).

When it says 'they left him and went away,' presumably they went away in frustration and annoyance—*failed again*! However, they had expressed the truth; Jesus was indeed a teacher who was not swayed by outward appearances. He was concerned with matters of the heart.

Later, Luke tells us about one particular Pharisee who would presumably have been opposed to Jesus, but who urged restraint in their opposition to the apostles. He said, 'If this plan or this undertaking is of man, it will fail; but if it is of God, you will not be able to overthrow them. You might even be found opposing God!' (Acts 5:38, 39). There again is the truth from an enemy of Christ; in opposing him and rejecting his great salvation, they were indeed opposing God; and, as Hebrews 2:3 asks, 'How shall we escape if we neglect such a great salvation?'

Another person who would be expected to be an enemy of Christ is the Jewish king Agrippa, to whom we referred earlier. Paul appeared before him, and from Agrippa's lips we hear some words of great irony. He heard Paul's 'true and rational words,' (Acts 26:25) but as he began to feel hot under the collar, he diverted Paul with his mocking words, 'In a short time would you persuade me to be a Christian?' (Acts 26:28). The words have been translated in various ways and Eugene Peterson perhaps catches the amused and dismissive thrust of Agrippa's words: 'Keep this up much longer and you'll make a Christian out of me!'[10] If things get too near to the bone, one can always crack a joke.

But Paul responded, 'Whether short or long, I would to God that not only you but also all who hear me this day might become such as I am,' adding (perhaps with a little twinkle in his eye), 'except for these chains.'

Agrippa was correct in his assertion that Paul wanted to convert him—although Paul would say it is only God who can convert people. Paul was simply his instrument, his ambassador, his evangelist, and he did indeed long for Agrippa and others to come to know the good news of the gospel. Agrippa spoke the truth about Paul's great desire—that people should 'come to a knowledge of the truth,' for, as Paul would later assert, 'There is one God, and there is one mediator between God and men, the man Christ Jesus, who gave himself as a ransom for all, which is the testimony given at the proper time' (1 Tim. 2:5, 6).

Many a true word

Many truths have been unintentionally expressed even by enemies of Christ and his gospel.

- He *does* welcome sinners
- No one *has* ever spoken like him
- He *did* die that others should not perish but have everlasting life
- He *is* truly the King

[10] Eugene Peterson, *The Message–The New Testament in Contemporary Language* (Colorado Springs: NavPress, 1993).

- He *did* save others and he *didn't* save himself at Golgotha
- He *did* come into the world to save sinners
- The name Christian *was* the right name
- His gospel *has* turned the world upside down
- The persecutor *did* become the preacher of Jesus and the resurrection

These are from different parts of the New Testament and we have considered them as unintended statements of saving truth.

2 Timothy 3:15-16 says that the Bible 'is able to make you wise for salvation through faith in Christ Jesus. All Scripture is breathed out by God and profitable for teaching, for reproof, for correction, and for training in righteousness', and my prayer is that the chapters of this book have prompted us to a renewed love for God's word in Scripture and for the holy and gracious Lord who speaks through it. The longest Psalm says in prayer to this great triune God, 'The unfolding of your words gives light' (Psa. 119:130).

One statement of Christian belief, which is accepted by many denominations of the church, says,

> The authority of the holy Scripture, for which it ought to be believed and obeyed, dependeth not upon the testimony of any man, or church, but wholly upon God (who is truth itself), the author thereof; and therefore it is to be received, because it is the word of God.

It also says,

> The whole counsel of God, concerning all things necessary for his own glory, man's salvation, faith, and life, is either expressly set down in scripture, or by good and necessary consequence may be deduced from scripture: unto which nothing at any time is to be added, whether by new revelations of the Spirit, or traditions of men.[11]

[11] *Westminster Confession of Faith*, Chapter 1, Paragraphs IV and VI.

The phrase in brackets—'who is truth itself'—is the foundational basis of Christianity. God has revealed himself to mankind, and the gospel is not a made-up story intended to produce happy feelings of comfort in a confusing world. Sir Francis Bacon famously wrote, '*What is truth?* said jesting Pilate, and would not stay for an answer,'[12] but Pilate's question (John 18:38) is the most basic question of all. The Bible claims to be the truth, as we see in the following verses, spoken not in jest or irony but by the inspiration of the Holy Spirit of God:

- 'I the Lord speak the truth; I declare what is right' (Isa. 45:19)
- 'God our Saviour desires all people to be saved and to come to the knowledge of the truth' (1 Tim. 2:14)
- 'Sanctify them in the truth; your word is truth' (John 17:17)
- 'The truth will set you free' (John 8:32)
- 'Jesus said, "I am the truth"' (John 14:6)

The gospel according to Christ

These words of Jesus are fundamental, and we end with *the gospel according to Christ*. It is of the greatest importance to hear from the Man himself about the purpose and effect of his coming.

So here, in conclusion, are ten things that Jesus specifically said about his own mission, the reason for his coming into the world:

1. John 6:38—'**I have come down from heaven, not to do my own will but the will of him who sent me.**' Jesus was not merely another in a long line of prophets, teachers or martyrs. The reality is that which finds expression in the Christmas hymn that says, 'He came down to earth from

---

[12] https://www.bartleby.com/3/1/1.html (accessed 11 May 2019).

heaven who is God and Lord of all.'[13] As is sometimes said, he came not only to preach the gospel (Mark 1:14) but also that there might be a gospel to preach. It is good news to be preached to all the world (Mark 13:10).

2. John 18:37—'**For this purpose I was born and for this purpose I have come into the world—to bear witness to the truth.**' Bethlehem did not mark the beginning of Jesus' existence but the coming into this world of One who truly *had* no beginning, the eternal Word. And the gospel is the truth of God.

3. Mark 2:17—'**I came not to call the righteous, but sinners.**' By 'the righteous' Jesus clearly meant people who *think* that they are righteous and assume that they have no need of forgiveness or salvation. The truth is that there *are* no such righteous people, and the big question is whether people are willing to confess their sinfulness and turn from it in repentance. Sin is an extremely unpopular concept. A university principal spoke about the awareness of it: 'With what eagerness we all clutch at these explanations (Oedipus complex etc.) which explain away our sense of responsibility! This is why atheism has a perennial appeal; it is wishful thinking in its most enticing form.'[14] But just as the recovery of good physical health involves facing up to whatever is causing the problem, our spiritual well-being begins with the recognition of the reality and seriousness of sin and its consequences.

4. Matthew 20:28—'**The Son of Man came not to be served**

---

[13] Hymn, 'Once in royal David's city' by Cecil Frances Alexander (1818–95).
[14] Sir Thomas Taylor, *Where One Man Stands* (Edinburgh: St Andrew Press, 1960), 24.

but to serve, and to give his life as a ransom for many.' Far from demanding that others serve him, he is the One who came to serve, as depicted in the incident when he took upon himself the task of a slave and washed the feet of his disciples (John 13:5). And his ultimate act of service was the sacrifice of his own life as a ransom, taking our sin upon himself, that he might offer a full salvation to all who will accept it from him in penitence and faith.

5. John 12:46—'**I have come into the world as light, so that whoever believes in me may not remain in darkness.**' This is the wonderful promise; we are not given to know the answers to all of our questions, but faith inspires the testimony, 'I looked to Jesus and I found in him my Star, my Sun, and in that light of life I'll walk till travelling days are done.'[15]

6. John 20:29—'**Blessed are those who have not seen and yet have believed.**' He calls for our faith now and he also promised that his people will eventually see him face to face. 'Without faith,' we are told, 'it is impossible to please him' (Heb. 11:6). Paul characterised the Christian life as a life of faith—'We walk by faith, not by sight' (2 Cor. 5:7) and this is in line with Jesus' invitation to put our faith in him (e.g. Mark 11:22).

7. John 10:10—'**I came that they may have life and have it abundantly.**' He not only came with a message of salvation from the power of death and hell but also to enrich life in this world. Charles Spurgeon told of a fellow-minister who, in days of widespread poverty, went to the house of

[15] Hymn, 'I heard the voice of Jesus' by Horatius Bonar (1808–89).

a poor person to give her some money to help her pay the rent. He knocked several times but got no answer. It transpired that the woman was at home, but, she said later, she heard the knocking but thought it was the rent-collector coming to demand payment.[16] The gospel according to Christ is news, not of rent demanded, but of rent paid. It is all about what he has done so that people may enter into fulness of life and gain eternal life. This is the importance of answering when he knocks at the door (Rev. 3:20).

8. Luke 19:10—'**The Son of Man came to seek and to save the lost**,' lost people like Zacchaeus to whom the words were first spoken. We referred earlier to Luke 15 which is a chapter of lost things: the lost sheep, the lost coin and the lost sons. It may not be flattering to be compared with a lost sheep, an inanimate coin, a prodigal son or a truculent brother, but the good news is that Christ came to seek the lost.

9. Luke 24:46, 47—'**It is written that the Christ should suffer and on the third day rise from the dead, and that repentance and forgiveness of sins should be proclaimed in his name to all nations**.' Paul spoke about God commanding all people everywhere to repent (Acts 17:30). Repentance means turning around and going in a different direction. It involves a change of mind, a change of heart and a change of priorities in life. And it starts with the attitude that says:

> Nothing in my hand I bring
> Simply to Thy cross I cling;
> Naked, come to Thee for dress;

---

[16] Recounted in John Baillie, *Invitation to Pilgrimage* (London: Oxford University Press, 1942), 48-9.

Helpless, look to Thee for grace;
Foul, I to the fountain fly;
Wash me, Saviour, or I die.[17]

10. John 3:16, 17—'**God so loved the world, that he gave his only Son, that whoever believes in him should not perish but have eternal life. For God did not send his Son into the world to condemn the world, but in order that the world might be saved through him.**' This is the gospel—according to Jesus.

---

[17] Hymn, 'Rock of Ages' by Augustus Montague Toplady (1740–78).

Epilogue:
The Things People Say!

This book has looked at the gospel according to Christ's enemies in the first century. What about our twenty-first century, in which we are bombarded constantly with such a variety of ideas and opinions? In our age of soundbites, social media, culture wars, cancel culture and no-platforming, are there instances of biblical truth being unintentionally expressed by opponents of the gospel?

Consider the following seven attitudes, which unwittingly express truths that their proponents don't intend.

The first is the assertion that **'Religion is the problem with the world, not the solution.'** This is intended as an attack on Christianity, but the critic might be surprised to hear Christians respond, 'We quite agree.'

It all depends, of course, on what is meant by 'religion.' For many people the word refers to a set of practices that are supposed to earn favour with a deity, the kind of religion described by one of my sons as a *try harder* religion. He refers to the children's story, *The Little Engine That Could*: 'The other engines say it's too hard to pull all the carriages up the hill but the little engine has a go. As he strains and strains and slowly climbs, he says to himself, over and over, "I think I can, I think I can, I think I can…" That's what 'religion' is like. That's what non-Christian ethics is like. Can I do better? Can I improve? Can I climb this moral mountain? I think I can, I think I can…'[1]

Critics of religion sometimes point to examples of the harm done or defended by it—things like slavery, religious wars and the Inquisition. When the enemies of Christ express this criticism, Christians can only agree—but also assert that it is not the *Christian* religion that is the problem, and that Christianity isn't really a 'religion' at all. It is rather a relationship of faith and love with the gracious God revealed in Scripture, faith and love which express themselves in thankful worship, holy living and practical care for other people.

In a doorstep conversation once with some Jehovah's Witnesses I was asked, 'What benefit do you have from thinking of God as a Trinity?' The question may have been little more than an opening gambit (an attempt to keep me from shutting the door on them!), but my response was to say that such 'benefit' is not the point. The question implies that Christianity is a system that we have devised, invented or thought out, but I was at pains to argue that real Christianity is about *the God who is there* (as Francis Schaeffer entitled one of his books), that Christianity is about God's self-revelation and that our part is to respond to what he has revealed to us.

No-one can claim that Christianity has an unblemished track-record; Christians have often been poor ambassadors for Christ and have erred. But it is true (the gospel according to Christ's enemies) that 'religion' has often been the problem, not

[1] Andrew M. Randall, *Following Jesus* (Edinburgh: Banner of Truth, 2018), 86.

the solution. However the gospel is good news of something far better than a religion; it is good news of a Saviour who calls us to follow him.

* * *

Another line of attack says, '**Christians are no better than anyone else.**' It is an accusation which implies that Christians think they are superior to others! In fact, however, we make no such claim. We could simply accept this criticism and say that it's true! Far from thinking or proclaiming ourselves to be better than other people, Christians admit their flaws and sins, and trust in the undeserved grace of God who does not treat us as our sins deserve (Psa. 103:10), but who has acted for our salvation.

If people say that it's the church that puts them off Christianity, we should reply that it is Christ, not Christians, to whom we point and to whom they need to respond. Christians should be the most humble of people—not with a false or pretended humility, but with a genuine humility which acknowledges that we owe everything to Christ.

Think of the characters in the Bible, the raw material that God was working on. It's quite a list:

- Noah got drunk (Gen. 9:21)
- Abraham lied (Gen. 12:13)
- Sarah laughed at God's promise (Gen. 12:12)
- Jacob was a schemer (Gen. 27:19)
- Moses killed a man (Exod. 2:12)
- Rahab was a prostitute (Josh. 6:17)
- Samson was a womaniser (Judges 16:1)

- David committed adultery and murder (2 Sam. 11:4, 15)

- Jonah tried to run away from God (Jon. 1:3)

- The Samaritan woman had been divorced several times (John 4:16-18)

- Peter denied Christ (John 18:17)

- Thomas doubted (John 20:25)

- Paul persecuted Christians (Acts 9:1)

- Euodia and Syntyche were at loggerheads (Phil. 4:2)

- Barnabas and Saul had a sharp disagreement (Acts 15:39)

Paul emphasised the glory of the gospel, but he also wrote, 'we have this treasure in jars of clay, to show that the surpassing power belongs to God and not to us.' (2 Cor. 4:7)

Jesus spoke about building his church on the foundation of faith in him as the Son of the living God (Matt. 16:18), and Paul would later address the Christians of Ephesus, 'You also are being built together into a dwelling place for God by the Spirit' (Eph. 2:22).

How would we respond to someone who looked at a building site and complained about all the mess that could be seen there—piles of bricks lying about, stacks of timber, various vehicles cluttering the place? We would say, 'But the job isn't finished yet. There may be a mess now, but when the work is finished, everything will be tidied up and there will be a new house, with everything spick and span.'

The church is God's building site; he is still working on his church and it will not be completed until the end. Christ's call is addressed to ordinary, imperfect sinners, and it takes time for such characters to be moulded according to the pattern of Christ. It is Christ and his wonderful gospel that we seek to proclaim, not ourselves. As John the Baptist said, 'He must increase, but I must decrease' (John 3:30).

* * *

Another thing that is said by our opponents is **'Christianity is a crutch.'** If the accusation were that Christianity is *merely* a crutch, then we could not agree with it, but the sentiment that Christianity is a crutch gives an unintentional expression to a wonderful aspect of the gospel.

For someone who has suffered an injury, a crutch is a very helpful thing; it enables that person to move about in a way that would not be possible otherwise. And the Bible's message is that we are all metaphorically lame or crippled. That being so, the gospel is a wonderful blessing. It says that God 'gives power to the faint, and to him who has no might he increases strength' (Isa. 40:29).

Far from such assurances being 'merely a crutch', they speak of the sympathy and kindness of a good God who gives strength to weak sinners who look to him in penitence and faith. We all labour under the burden of sin, and many people also are crippled because of things that have happened—illness, disease, natural disaster, violence, atrocity, bereavement. The gospel of Jesus, which some would dismiss as *merely a crutch*, does address such issues. The message of God's salvation assures those who accept it (or accept *him*) that nothing can separate us from the love of Christ (Rom. 8:38-39) and that his grace is sufficient for our every need (2 Cor. 12:9).

It may be said as a dismissive criticism—Christianity is a crutch—but it does point to something wonderfully true. The gospel invitation is to 'Ask the Saviour to help you, comfort, strength and keep you; he is willing to aid you; he will carry you through.'[2]

* * *

'Christianity is for simple people' is another example of the gospel being expressed by Christ's enemies. It is intended as a criticism, implying that the gospel only appeals to unthinking or unsophisticated people, but we would agree with it; Christianity *is* for simple people.

When Jesus had miraculously given sight to a man who had been blind from birth, people couldn't believe that the sighted man was the very one who used to sit at the roadside begging. They asked his parents, who simply said that they didn't understand what had happened, but, 'Ask him; he is of age. He will speak for himself.' They did so and the man said that there were many things he couldn't understand, but 'one thing I do know, that though I was blind, now I see' (John 9:25).

The story goes on to tell of the man finding out more about Jesus and becoming one of his followers. As someone who had been blind from birth he would have received little, if any, education. In a sense, therefore, he was a simple person, and he illustrates this theme that the gospel is indeed for simple people. Of course it is not *only* for simple people, but thankfully faith and discipleship do not depend on the level of one's education or intellect.

* * *

Strangely, the opposite attitude is also sometimes expressed as a criticism of the Christian message; some suppose that **'Christianity is for intellectuals.'** The idea is that Christianity is for

---

[2] Refrain of hymn, 'Yield not to temptation' by Horatio Richmond Palmer, (1834–1907).

sophisticated and educated people and not for simple folk. Much that has been said already also applies here, and again as Christians we agree with the sentiment. Christianity is indeed for intellectuals—the criticism is valid! The problem with this and the previous topic only really arises if the word 'just' is inserted, that is, if it were being asserted that 'Christianity is *only* for simple people' or '*only* for intellectuals.' The gospel is for all kinds of people, and our IQ has nothing to do with it!

John Lennox has recounted an interesting story from his time as a student at Cambridge University: 'I found myself at a formal college dinner sitting beside a Nobel Prize winner. I had never met a scientist of such distinction before and … in order to gain the most from the conversation, I asked him whether his wide-ranging studies had led him to reflect on the existence of God.'

He says that the scientist was not comfortable with such a question, but later he invited a few people back to his study and in discussion asked, 'Lennox, do you want a career in science?' When Lennox said that he did, the scientist went on, 'Then in front of witnesses, tonight you must give up this childish faith in God. If you do not, then it will cripple you intellectually and you will suffer by comparison with your peers. You simply will not make it.'[3]

Since then, John Lennox has had an illustrious career and is now Emeritus Professor of Mathematics and Emeritus Fellow in Mathematics and the Philosophy of Science at the University of Oxford. It seems that he did 'make it'! Christianity certainly *is* for intellectuals!

* * *

---

[3] John Lennox, *Can Science Explain Everything?* (Oxford: The Good Book Company, 2019), 14-15.

Another attack on Christianity says that **Christians are intolerant.** They say, 'Tolerance should be our goal'—and again we would agree, although it depends on what is meant by tolerance.

Once, it simply meant an attitude of respect for other people and their views; if two people had conflicting views they could agree to differ and respect each other. Tolerance of that kind is a great thing, but for many people today, tolerance has come to mean the acceptance of views with which you disagree as equal to your own, never claiming that our view is truer or better than anyone else's, and we should certainly not attempt to change anyone's mind.

So Christians—who claim that Christ is not only a pointer to the truth, or an aspect of the truth, but *the Truth* (John 14:6)— are regarded as intolerant, and the assertion that tolerance should be our goal means that such truth claims should not be tolerated.

This view is well illustrated in the words of a teacher in a Scottish secondary school who was describing a course on the world's major religions. She said that the main emphasis of any religious studies is on the premise that everyone's viewpoint is valid. Really? Does that include the viewpoints of terrorists who kill innocent people, fraudsters who cheat others, paedophiles who abuse children?

Christians are all for tolerance in the proper sense of respect and kindness; we are also all for spreading the gospel of Jesus Christ, 'the way, and the truth, and the life' (John 14:6).

* * *

Similarly, opponents of Christianity sometimes say something like, '**We just need more of Jesus' teaching about loving one another,**' and who would argue against that? Back in the 1960s there was a popular song which expressed the view that what the

world needs is love, and for many people, that is the essence of
Jesus' teaching and they like to think of him as a nice man going
about in the Galilean sunshine encouraging people to be nice to
each other.

Obviously love does feature strongly in Jesus' teaching, and
we can only agree with the sentiment that the world needs more
love. But this assertion is often a veiled attack on Christian doctrine, the theology which they would say obscures the plain message of, say, the Sermon on the Mount.

This view was typified by Dr John MacArthur when he referred
to a newspaper clipping which someone had sent him. It was
a letter to the editor of an Australian newspaper about a Billy
Graham mission there. The letter-writer said that he was heartily
sick of the type of religion that insists our souls needs saving. He
wrote, 'I have never felt that I was lost. Nor do I feel that I daily
wallow in the mire of sin, although repetitive preaching insists
that I do. Give me a practical religion that teaches gentleness
and tolerance, that acknowledges no barriers of colour or creed,
that remembers the aged and teaches children of goodness and
not sin. If in order to save my soul I must accept such a philosophy as I have recently heard preached, I prefer to remain forever
damned.[4]

Many people would echo that 'give me a practical religion that
teaches gentleness and tolerance' rather than all the other parts of
the Bible's message. MacArthur's comment is, 'A sad letter. But
the truth is, that man understood the stark choices. He just made
the wrong one.'

Christians are all for making the world a better, nicer place,
but the Bible's message is a realistic one that takes account of

[4] John MacArthur, *The Gospel According to Jesus* (Grand Rapids: Zondervan,
1989), 186.

the reality and consequences of sin, the obvious fact that human effort has consistently failed to create utopia on this earth. And that isn't God's fault! As the prophet Isaiah wrote, the world's problems do not lie with God, but with human beings: 'The Lord's hand is not shortened, that it cannot save, or his ear dull, that it cannot hear; but your iniquities have made a separation between you and your God, and your sins have hidden his face from you so that he does not hear' (Isa. 59:1-3).

And if it be asserted that these words come from the Old Testament, and not from the lips of the gentle Jesus, the fact is that Jesus also spoke very forthrightly about human sin and fallenness. In the very Sermon on the Mount which some people contrast with the doctrinal teaching found in the New Testament epistles, we find him saying, 'If you then who are evil, know how to give good gifts to your children, how much more will your Father who is in heaven give good things to those who ask him' (Matthew 7:11). The little phrase, 'who are evil' says it all: it points to the fundamental flaw in human beings, the fact that there is something dark and fallen in all of us.

In words already quoted, J. B. Phillips wrote, 'Jesus was no sentimental do-gooder and he spoke quite unequivocally about rewards and punishment "in the world to come."' Phillips described such words as 'some of the most terrifying words in the New Testament,' yet they are not threats or menaces but 'warnings given in deadly earnest by the incarnation of unsentimental love.'[5]

So, if enemies of Christianity say that what is needed is more of Jesus' teaching about loving one another, they are speaking

---

[5] J. B. Phillips, *Ring of Truth—A Translator's Testimony* (London: Hodder & Stoughton, 1967), 68.

the truth but not the whole truth. The whole truth is that in our fallen condition we are guilty before God and we need his salvation from the guilt and power of sin, and we need his power to live out the truths he has taught us.

* * *

The gospel according to Christ's enemies has been expressed in many ways in ancient days and in modern or postmodern (or even post-postmodern) times. Often these statements point to God's truth. He *does* welcome sinners, he *has* spoken matchless words. He *did* die in the place of others. He *is* the King, he came to save sinners, to turn the world upside down.

And still his invitation stands, the most wonderful truth: 'God so loved the world, that he gave his only son, that whoever believes in him should not perish but have eternal life.' (John 3:16)

'The head that once was crowned with thorns
Is crowned with glory now.'

Thomas Kelly (1769–1854)

Also by David J. Randall

A Sad Departure
Why we could not stay in the Church of Scotland

'...a thoughtful, honest and solemnising book written out of a deep personal and practical concern for the cause of the gospel.'
— Sinclair Ferguson

'a significant work on a contemporary Christian scandal.'
—*Evangelical Times*

'...a lucid manifesto explaining why he and others [have left] the Church of Scotland ... equally true and compelling for any believer or pastor in any denomination or association whose official doctrine declares a departure from the word of God, written and incarnate.'
—John MacArthur

ISBN 978 1 84871 661 2 | 216pp. | paperback

BANNER *of* **TRUTH**

THE Banner of Truth Trust originated in 1957 in London. The founders believed that much of the best literature of historic Christianity had been allowed to fall into oblivion and that, under God, its recovery could well lead not only to a strengthening of the church, but to true revival.

Inter-denominational in vision, this publishing work is now international, and our lists include a number of contemporary authors along with classics from the past. The translation of these books into many languages is encouraged.

A monthly magazine, *The Banner of Truth*, is also published. More information about this and all our publications can be found on our website or supplied by either of the offices below.

Head Office:
3 Murrayfield Road
Edinburgh
EH12 6EL, United Kingdom
Email: info@banneroftruth.co.uk

North America Office:
PO Box 621
Carlisle, PA 17013
United States of America
Email: info@banneroftruth.org